Welcome to Chang'an,
a World-Famous
Ancient Capital

李 栋　王 向 辉　编著

千年古都　常来长安

Compiled by
Li Dong
Wang Xianghui

西安出版社
Xi'an Publishing House

图书在版编目（CIP）数据

千年古都　常来长安 / 李栋, 王向辉编著 . — 西安:
西安出版社, 2021.7
ISBN 978-7-5541-5541-7

Ⅰ.①千… Ⅱ.①李…②王… Ⅲ.①西安—概况—
图集 Ⅳ.①K924.11-64.

中国版本图书馆CIP数据核字(2021)第150837号

Cataloguing in Publication (CIP) Data
Welcome to Chang'an, a World-Famous Ancient Capital/Compiled by: Li Dong, Wang Xianghui — Xi'an:
Xi'an Publishing House, July 2021
ISBN 978-7-5541-5541-7
I.①Thousand... II.①Li...②Wang... III.①Xi'an-Overview IV.①K924.II-64
Archival Library of Chinese Publications CIP Data HZ (2021) No. 150837

千年古都　常来长安
QIAN NIAN GU DU　CHANG LAI CHANG'AN

Welcome to Chang'an, a World-Famous Ancient Capital

编　著：李栋　王向辉	Compiled by: Li Dong, Wang Xianghui
策划统筹：卜杰　贺勇华	Schemed and coordinated by: Bu Jie, He Yonghua
图片统筹：陈群　刘珂　薛铂　张颖博	Photo coordinators: Chen Qun, Liu Ke, Xue Bo, Zhang Yingbo
翻译统筹：王卫强	Translator: Wang Weiqiang
责任编辑：李丹　路索	Editors in charge: Li Dan, Lu Suo
特约编辑：范婷婷	Contributing editor: Fan Tingting
责任校对：张增兰	Proofreader in charge: Zhang Zenglan
封面设计：飞洋设计机构　郭超	Cover designer: Feiyang Design Agency, Guo Chao
内文套版：西安纸尚图文	Text overprinting by: Xi'an Zhishang Graphic Design
印刷统筹：尹苗	Printing coordinator: Yin Miao
出版发行：西安出版社	Published and distributed by: Xi'an Publishing House
电　话：029-85253740	Tel.: 029-85253740
印　刷：陕西龙山海天艺术印务有限公司	Printed by: Shaanxi Longshan Haitian Art Printing Co., Ltd.
开　本：787mm×1092mm 1/16	Book size: 787mm×1092mm 1/16
印　张：17.75	Sheet: 17.75
字　数：290 千字	Character count: 290 thousand
版　次：2021 年 7 月第 1 版	Edition: 1st edition in July 2021
印　次：2021 年 8 月第 1 次印刷	Number of print: 1st printing in August 2021
书　号：ISBN 978-7-5541-5541-7	Book No. : ISBN 978-7-5541-5541-7
定　价：98.00 元	Price: 98.00 RMB yuan

目录
CONTENTS

长安回望绣成堆

　　西安，古称长安，是陕西省省会，雄踞关中平原中部，北望苍莽的黄土高原，南依巍峨大秦岭，泾河、渭河、浐河、灞河、沣河、滈河、潏河、涝河环绕，构成"八水绕长安"的秀丽山川。

　　长安回望绣成堆，山顶千门次第开。

　　西安是一座有三千多年建城史，一千多年建都史的历史文化名城。千载中国的历史巅峰周、秦、汉、唐在这里演绎无数的悲欢离合。周丰镐遗址，秦始皇兵马俑，汉未央宫、长乐宫，唐大明宫、兴庆宫，明城墙，记录着这座城市岁月长河中的绝代风华，"西罗马，东长安"并称为文明的双子星座，西安作为中华民族的精神家园，是中国文化的坐标之城之一。

　　西安是一座文化之城。李白、杜甫、王维、白居易在这里咏月吟风；吴道子、阎立本在这里笔落风雨；孙思邈在这里悬壶济世；李淳风、僧一行在这里遥望璀璨的星空……三千年，群星灿烂，熠熠生辉；三千年，藏龙卧虎，薪火相传。文学陕军、长安画派、黄土画派、易俗社、青曲社、西安电影制片厂……仍在新时代书写这座城市的文化传奇。

　　西安是一座宝藏之城，儒、释、道在这里开宗立派，学脉绵亘，历代的文物流光溢彩。

　　西安是一座革命之城，葛牌镇区苏维埃政府、西安事变旧址、八路军西安办事处等，红色旗帜在这里迎风招展，铭刻着先烈们的碧血丹心。

西安是一座开放之城。这里是丝绸之路的起点，国家中心城市，东西方文明交融的开放高地，张骞、鉴真、鸠摩罗什、阿倍仲麻吕，无数的友好使者，跨越浩瀚大漠，无边的海洋，让这座城与世界相连，万国衣冠，盛世繁华，仍然在城市的角落中鲜活。

西安是一座科教之城。教育资源位居全国前三，航空、航天、半导体等高科技优势突出，杨森、华为、三星、陕汽、陕鼓、比亚迪、吉利一路披荆斩棘，现代化的西安，依然闪亮。

西安是一座幸福之城，碧水蓝天、宜居宜业，连续九年获得中国最具幸福感城市荣誉称号。追赶超越、不忘初心，在中华民族的伟大复兴中，这座城如一只美丽的凤凰，正在展翅腾飞。

Looking back from Chang'an
a heap of rich brocade on Mount Lishan I saw

Xi'an, called Chang'an in ancient times, is the capital of Shaanxi Province. It occupies the central part of Guanzhong Plain, with the vast Loess Plateau to the north and the majestic Qinling Mountains on the south. The eight rivers of Jinghe, Weihe, Chanhe River, Bahe, Fenghe, Haohe, Juehe and Laohe encircle the city of Chang'an, which constitutes a enchanting landscape of the city.

Looking back from Chang'an, a heap of rich brocade on Mount Lishan I saw; Thousands of palaces at its top, it seems, showed much grandeur and awe.

Xi'an is a famous cultural city with a history of over 3,000 years of city construction and over 1000 years of being a capital. Zhou, Qin, Han and Tang Dynasties, the peaks of China's history for thousands of years, staged countless joys and sorrows here. The Fenghao Ruins of Zhou Dynasty, Terracotta Warriors and Horses of Qin Shihuang, the First Emperor of Qin Dynasty, Weiyang Palace and Chang-le Palace of Han Dynasty, Daming Palace and Xingqing Palace of Tang Dynasty, and City Wall of Ming Dynasty all record the unparalleled elegance of the city. "Rome in the west and Chang'an in the east" are called the Gemini of human civilization. As the spiritual home of the Chinese nation, Xi'an is a city of coordinates of the Chinese culture.

Xi'an is a city of culture. Li Bai, Du Fu, Wang Wei, Bai Juyi and other poets once sang their romantic carols and songs here; Wu Daozi and Yan Liben once made their wonderful paintings here. Sun Simiao once practiced medicine here to help the public. Astrologer Li Chunfeng and astronomer Monk Yixing were once here to watch the stars ... For three thousand years, brilliant people have lived like stars shining brightly in the sky. For three thousand years, talented people have come to the fore, and passed on splendid heritage from generation to generation. Shaanxi Writers Group, Chang'an School of Painting, Loess School of Painting, Yisu Art Troupe and Shaanxi Opera, Shaanxi Youth Folk Art Club and Xi'an Film Studio are still creating cultural legends of the city in the new era.

Xi'an is a city of treasures. Confucianism, Buddhism and Taoism have long been established here. It enjoys a wide range of profound learning traditions and breathtaking cultural relics from all previous dynasties.

Xi'an is a revolutionary city, with the District Soviet Government site in Gepai Town, the former site of Xi'an Incident, the Eighth Route Army Xi'an Office, etc. where the red flag still unfurls in the wind and the loyalty and patriotism of the martyrs are carved on the stone.

Xi'an is an open city. It is the starting point of Silk Road, the national central city, and a vanguard of opening up to the outside world with the integration of eastern and western civilizations. It is also the place where countless friendly messengers such as Zhang Qian, Jian Zhen, Kumarajiva and Abe Nakamaro, having crossed the vast deserts or boundless seas, travelled to connect the city with other parts of the world, leaving a rich legacy that can still be felt in every corner of the city.

Xi'an is a city of science and education. Educational resources rank among the top three in the country, and high-tech technologies such as aviation, aerospace and semiconductor are unrivalled. Such companies as Janssen, Huawei, Samsung, Shaanxi Automobile, Shaanxi Blower, BYD and Geely have thrived from the very beginning in the increasingly modern city of Xi'an.

Xi'an is a happy city, with clear water, blue sky and comfortable livelihood. It has won the honorary title of the happiest city in China for nine years in a row. Still quickening its steps and always bearing in mind the original aspiration, this city is like a beautiful phoenix, spreading its wings and taking off.

山水秦岭　华夏祖脉

CHAPTER ONE QINLING MOUNTAINS:
AN ANCESTRAL VEIN OF THE CHINESE NATION

◀ 秦岭
Qinling Mountains

西安，踞关中平原腹地，北望黄土高原，南依秦岭山脉，黄河最大支流渭河横贯东西。依山握水的天人格局，使西安成为中国最早的山水之城。

秦岭，是长江和黄河流域的分水岭，秦岭—淮河一线成为我国暖温带与亚热带的分界线。长期以来，人们把秦岭—淮河一线看作是中国"南方"和"北方"的地理分界线。

秦岭是我国的"中央水塔"，是陕西最重要的水源涵养区域，史有"八水绕长安"的恢宏胜景，也是我国最重要的生态安全屏障、种子植物"基因库"，有"秦岭无闲草"的美誉。秦岭是植物的乐土，也是野生动物的天堂，有国家一级保护动物13种、二级保护动物58种，其中大熊猫、金丝猴、羚牛、朱鹮被誉为"秦岭四宝"，以它们为原型设计的熊熊、金金、羚羚、朱朱是中华人民共和国第十四届运动会吉祥物。

● 秦岭雪景
Snow Scene of Qinling Mountains

Xi'an is located in the heartland of Guanzhong (central Shaanxi) Plain, bordering the Loess Plateau in the north and the Qinling Mountains in the south. The Weihe River, the largest tributary of the Yellow River, runs through the whole city from west to east. Xi'an is the earliest city in China that is famous for its landscapes due to its superior geographical conditions.

The Qinling Mountains is the watershed between the Yangtze River and the Yellow River. The Qinling-Huaihe line divides warm temperate zone and subtropical zone in China. For a long time, the Qinling-Huaihe line has been regarded as the geographical dividing line between China's "South" and "North".

As a "central water tower," the Qinling Mountains is the most significant area for water conservation in Shaanxi, providing water supply for the splendid view of the "eight rivers around Chang'an". It is the most important ecological shelter in China and a gene pool for seed plants, hence the reputation of "no idle grass in the Qinling Mountains". The mountains are a paradise for wild animals as well as plants. There are 13 kinds of national first-class protected animals and 58 kinds of second-class protected animals, among which giant pandas, golden monkeys, takins and crested ibis are known as the "four treasures of the Qinling Mountains", and they are mascots of the 14th National Games, bearing such names as Xiong Xiong, Jin Jin, Ling Ling and Zhu Zhu, respectively.

试登秦岭望秦川

Climbing up Qinling Mountains to Enjoy the Landscape

秦岭如母亲，将西安安放在它巨大而温暖的怀抱之中。终南山及其支脉翠华山、南五台、王顺山、骊山等群山青翠，使得西安城这幅山水画卷如有一道通天的镇尺，让这座城能怡然自得地在人间享受这岁月静好。

● 终南山雾海
Fog on Mount Zhongnan

The Qinling Mountains, like a mother, places Xi'an in its huge and warm embrace. The mountains of Zhongnan and its branch range of Cuihua, South Wutai, Wangshun, Lishan, all fresh and green, stand abreast like a heavenly paperweight for this landscape scroll of Xi'an so that the city can enjoy peace and harmony in the world to its heart's content.

终南山

Mount Zhongnan

终南山，又名地肺山、中南山、周南山，简称南山，位于西安城南，是中国重要的地理标志之一。它东起西安市蓝田县最东端的杨家堡，西至周至县最西界的秦岭主峰太白山，太白山拔仙台海拔 3771.2 米，是秦岭最高峰。终南山东西长约 230 千米，最宽处 55 千米，最窄处 15 千米，总面积约 4851 平方千米，横跨蓝田县、长安区、鄠邑区、周至县等西安所辖县区。终南山是国家 AAAA 级旅游景区、国家森林公园、国家自然保护区。2009 年 8 月 23 日，秦岭终南山入选世界地质公园。

终南山不仅占据重要的地理区位，还拥有得天独厚的人文资源。《诗经·小雅·天保》唱诵："如月之恒，如日之升。如南山之寿，不骞不崩。"寿比南山不老松，所说的南山，当是终南山无疑。武则天时代的卢藏用曾隐居于终南山，以假装避世求取功名获得成功，因此为后世留下了"终南捷径"的成语。

终南阴岭秀，积雪浮云端。
林表明霁色，城中增暮寒。
——【唐】祖咏《终南望余雪》

终南山雪景 ⬥
Snow Scene of Mount Zhongnan

Mount Zhongnan, also known as Difeishan, Zhongnanshan and Zhounanshan, or Nanshan (literally southern mountain) for short, is located in the south of Xi'an and is an important geographical symbol of China. It starts from Yangjiabao, the easternmost part of Lantian County, Xi'an, and ends at Mount Taibai, the highest peak of the Qinling Mountains in the westernmost part of Zhouzhi County. Mount Taibai is 3,771.2 meters above sea level, plus its highest point Baxiantai. Mount Zhongnan is about 230 kilometers long from east to west, 55 kilometers at its widest point and 15 kilometers at its narrowest point, with a total area of about 4,851 square kilometers. It spans Lantian County, Chang'an District, Huyi District, Zhouzhi County and other counties under the jurisdiction of Xi'an. It is a national AAAA-level scenic spot, a national forest park and a national nature reserve. On August 23, 2009, Mount Zhongnan in the Qinling Mountains was selected as the World Geopark.

Mount Zhongnan not only occupies an important geographical location, but also has unique humanistic resources. One of Minor Elegant Songs of Tianbao from The Book of Songs sings: "Like the constant moon, like the rising sun, wish you to live like the mountain long". When one makes a wish, words like "live as long as the pine tree on the southern mountain" are often said. Here the mountain undoubtedly refers to Mount Zhongnan. Lu Zangyong lived in the Zhongnan mountains in Empress Wu Zetian's time in Tang Dynasty, and succeeded in seeking fame by pretending to live a sequestered life. Therefore, he left behind an idiom of "Shortcut of the Southern Mountain" for later generations.

翠华山
Mount Cuihua

翠华山是终南山支脉，有"终南独秀"的美誉。其海拔2132米，面积1785公顷。翠华山风景区山崩地貌类型之全、保存之完整典型，为国内罕见，因此被称为"中国地质地貌博物馆"。

因峪口有汉武帝元封二年（前109）修建的太乙宫，传说太乙真人在此山修炼，又名太乙山。历经周秦汉唐，多次被辟为皇家"上林苑""御花园"。秦始皇嬴政曾在此狩猎休憩；汉武帝曾在此设立祭天道场，拜谒太乙神；秦圣宫是唐王李世民避暑消夏行宫。

太乙近天都，连山接海隅。
白云回望合，青霭入看无。
分野中峰变，阴晴众壑殊。
欲投人处宿，隔水问樵夫。
——【唐】王维《终南山》

翠华山
Mount Cuihua

Mount Cuihua is a branch of Mount Zhongnan, and has the reputation of "outshining other mountains". It is 2,132 meters above sea level and covers an area of 1,785 hectares. Mount Cuihua Scenic Area is rare in China because of its complete and well-preserved landscape types, so it is called "Geology and Geomorphology Museum of China".

Because there is Taiyi Palace built in the second year of Yuanfeng Period of Emperor Wudi of Han Dynasty (109 B.C.) at the valley entrance, it is said that Immortal Taiyi practiced on this mountain, hence the name Mount Taiyi. After Zhou, Qin, Han and Tang Dynasties, it was turned into "Shanglin Garden" and "Royal Garden" many times. Emperor Qin Shihuang of Qin Dynasty, Ying Zheng, once hunted and rested here, Emperor Wudi of Han Dynasty once established a Taoist temple to worship the God Taiyi, and Qinsheng Palace was once a summer palace for Li Shimin, Emperor of Tang Dynasty.

南五台为终南山支脉，《关中通志》说，"今南山神秀之区，惟长安南五台为最"。因山有观音、文殊、清凉、灵应、舍身5个山峰，又位于西安北部铜川市耀州区的五台山（药王山）以南，而得名南五台。

南五台自然风景颇佳，从山下看5座山峰如笔架排列，一览无余。南五台山重水复，峰回路转，险峰秀岩，目不暇接。涓流如帛的流水石瀑布，孤峰独秀的送灯台，峻拔凌霄的观音台，势若天柱的灵应台，惟妙惟肖的犀牛石，大自然神作连理枝等共同构成了南五台美不胜收的如画景色。

南五台是佛教圣地之一，山中有圣寿寺，圣寿寺塔建于隋代，方形7层，高23米。在圣寿寺塔北约50米处，有被后人尊为净土宗十三祖印光法师影堂石塔。

中峰曾到处，题记没苍苔。
振锡传深谷，翻经想旧台。
危松临砌偃，惊鹿蓦溪来。
内殿御诗切，身回心未回。
——【唐】司空图《次韵和秀上人游南五台》

Mount South Wutai is a branch of Mount Zhongnan. As General Annals of Shaanxi records, "The most beautiful area in Nanshan (southern mountains) is Mount South Wutai in Chang'an". Because the mountain has five peaks of Guanyin, Wenshu, Qingliang, Lingying and Shesheng, and is located to the south of Mount Wutai (Mount Yaowang) in Yaozhou District, Tongchuan City, to the north of Xi 'an, it is named South Wutai.

The natural scenery of Mount South Wutai is quite beautiful. Seen from the foot of the mountain, five peaks are arranged like a brush rack,. Mount South Wutai has numerous peaks and waters, winding paths along the mountain ridges, and beautiful rocks. The flowing waterfall on the smooth stone surface, the unique peak of light-sending platform, the towering peak of Guanyin platform, the pillar-like peak of Linying platform are tourist attractions. The lifelike rhinoceros stone, together with many other scenic spots, constitute the beautiful picturesque scenery of Mount South Wutai.

Mount South Wutai is one of the holy places of Buddhism.There is Shengshou Temple in the mountains. The Tower of Shengshou Temple was built in Sui Dynasty, with seven floors and a height of 23 meters. About 50 meters north of Shengshou Temple Tower, there is a stone tower in which the image of the thirteenth ancestors of the Pure Land Sect of Buddhism is displayed.

楼观台
Louguantai

　　楼观台又称"说经台"，位于陕西省周至县城东南15千米的终南山北麓。传说大圣人老子曾在此讲授《道德经》，是中国道文化的发祥之地，素有"天下第一福地"和"仙都"之称。宋代苏轼游此吟有名句："此台一览秦川小。"

　　楼观台不远处有重阳宫，为道教全真派祖庭，金庸先生小说《射雕英雄传》中的五绝之首王重阳就是全真派创派祖师，全真七子皆在重阳宫修持。《神雕侠侣》中小龙女居住的活死人墓就在重阳宫附近。

鸟噪猿呼昼闭门，寂寥谁识古皇尊。

青牛久已辞辕轭，白鹤时来访子孙。

——【宋】苏轼《自清平镇游楼观五郡大秦延生仙游往返四日得》（节选）

▼ 秦岭脚下的楼观花海
A Sea of Flowers of Louguantai at the Foot of Qinling Mountains

Louguantai, also known as "Shuojingtai" (meaning "preaching terrace"), is located at the northern foot of Mount Zhongnan, 15 kilometers southeast of Zhouzhi County, Shaanxi Province. Legend has it that Lao-Tsu, a great sage, once taught Tao Te Ching here in Louguantai, which is the birthplace of Chinese Tao culture and has long been known as the "first blessed land in the world" and the "celestial capital". In Song Dynasty, Su Shi visited this very site and wrote, "All the Shaanxi Plain can be held in a single glance when you reach the top of Louguantai."

Not far from Louguantai lies Chongyang Palace, which is the ancestral temple of Taoist Quanzhen Sect. Wang Chongyang, the first of the five kung fu masters in Mr. Jin Yong's novel Legend of the Condor Heroes, is the founder of Quanzhen Sect, and all the seven disciples of Quanzhen Sect once did Toist practice here in Chongyang Palace. The tomb of the living dead where Little Dragon Maiden is said to have lived in The Return of the Condor Heroes is near Chongyang Palace.

王顺山
Mount Wangshun

王顺山古称玉山。位于西安市蓝田县，距蓝田县城 20 千米，是秦岭终南山世界地质公园的重要组成部分。传说八仙中的韩湘子在玉山得道成仙。

玉山山畔是著名的蓝关古道，在从长安被贬潮州的途中，唐代大诗人韩愈为后世留下了"云横秦岭家何在？雪拥蓝关马不前"的千古诗句。明朝诗人刘玑也有诗赞叹玉山是"天下名山此独奇，望中风景画中诗"。

蓝水远从千涧落，玉山高并两峰寒。
——【唐】杜甫《九日蓝田崔氏庄》（节选）

Mount Wangshun was called Mount Yushan (meaning Jade Mountain) in ancient times. Located in Lantian County, Xi'an, 20 kilometers away from Lantian County seat, it is an important part of Mount Zhongnan World Geopark in Qinling Mountains. Legend has it that Han Xiangzi, one of the Eight Immortals, became immortal in Mount Yushan.

On the hillside of Mount Yushan is a famous ancient road of Languan (meaning Blue Pass). On the way from Chang'an to Chaozhou, Han Yu, a great poet of Tang Dynasty, left an eternal poem for later generations, which reads "Where is my home when clouds drift above the Qingling Mountains? My horse refuses to move ahead while heavy snow blocks the Blue Pass road". Liu Ji, a poet of Ming Dynasty, also praised Mount Yushan as "Among all famous mountains in the world Yushan is the most fascinating, looking like a painting in sight and a poem in painting".

王顺山秋景 ▶
Autumn Scenery of Mount Wangshun

骊山
Mount Lishan

骊，本义是黑色的马。骊山山势逶迤，树木葱茏，因远望宛如一匹苍黛色的骏马而得名。骊山位于西安市临潼区城南，由东西绣岭组成，满披青松翠柏，郁郁苍苍。每当夕阳西下，云霞满天，苍山绣岭涂上万道红霞，景色妩媚动人，这一景被誉为"骊山晚照"，是著名的关中八景之一。

传说女娲在这里"炼石补天"；周幽王在此以"烽火戏诸侯"断送了西周天下。在骊山脚下，千古一帝秦始皇以兵马俑和恢宏的陵墓做着自己的永世皇帝梦；唐玄宗与杨贵妃在骊山华清池许下了"在天愿作比翼鸟，在地愿为连理枝"的爱情誓言。1936年张学良、杨虎城在骊山发动西安事变，对蒋介石进行"兵谏"。骊山因此被誉为扭转乾坤的名山。

骊山绝望幸，花萼罢登临。
地下无朝烛，人间有赐金。
——【唐】杜甫《骊山》（节选）

The original meaning of "Li" is black horse. Mount Lishan is famous for its overlapping mountains and verdant trees, and looks like a beautiful horse with pale black color viewed from afar. Mount Lishan is located in the south of Lintong District, Xi'an. It is composed of east and west hills, covered with green pines and cypresses. Whenever the sun sets, clouds are all over the sky, tens of thousands of red glows are cast on the hills, and the scenery is charming and enchanting. This scenery, known as the "Evening Glow of Mount Lishan", is one of the eight attractions in Guanzhong, the central part of Shaanxi Province.

骊山晚照 ⬡
Evening Sunglow on Mount Lishan

In 1936, Zhang Xueliang and Yang Hucheng detained Chiang Kai-shek at today's Remonstrance Pavilion of Mount Lishan and launched the Xi'an Incident. Mount Lishan was therefore known as a famous mountain to reverse the course of events at the critical moment in Chinese history.

荡荡八水绕长安

Eight Rivers Encircling the City of Chang'an

西安境内河流以黄河流域的渭河水系为主，较大的河流有渭河、泾河、浐河、灞河、沣河、涝河、潏河、滈河。司马相如在《上林赋》中描述"终始灞浐，出入泾渭；酆镐潦潏，纡馀委蛇，经营乎其内。荡荡乎八川分流，相背而异态"。八水绕长安，哺育了周秦汉唐的盛世基业。汤汤北走，汇聚成川，浐灞合水，潏滈交汇，沣涝并行，与渭泾二河，共同织就了"天下陆海之地"的生态基底，营造出"八水绕长安"的胜景。

黑河金盆水库供应西安的约七成用水，成为维系西安生活、生产、生态可持续发展的重要命脉。

"三月三日天气新，长安水边多丽人"。如今历史上著名的昆明池、曲江池、渼陂湖等水系，生态也得到了恢复，让西安这座山水之城更加漾绿摇翠，清新动人。

黑河金盆水库 ⬠
Golden Basin Reservoir on Heihe River

In Xi'an, the Weihe River system of the Yellow River Basin plays a major role, and the larger rivers are Weihe, Jinghe, Chanhe, Bahe, Fenghe, Laohe, Juehe and Haohe. Sima Xiangru, a writer of Western Han Dynasty, described the rivers in his masterpiece "Ode to Shanglin Garden": "The Bahe River and Chanhe River both begin and end within the garden; the Jinghe River and the Weihe River flow in and out of it; and rivers of Fenghe, Haohe, Laohe and Juehe wind across it. The eight rivers flow abreast, following thier own ways and taking on different looks." The eight rivers around Chang'an have nurtured the prosperity of Zhou, Qin, Han and Tang dynasties. They flow north, merging into each other or moving ahead shoulder to shoulder, which weaves the ecological network of "land and water in the world" and creates a beautiful landscape of "Eight Rivers around Chang'an".

The Golden Basin Reservoir of the Heihe River, which supplies 70% of the water use in Xi'an, has become the strategic lifeline to maintain its livelihood, production and sustainable ecological development.

"On the third day of the third lunar month, in the freshening weather, more beauties can be seen by the waterside in Chang'an". Now, The famous water systems such as Kunming Pond, Qujiang Pond and Meibei Lake have also been ecologically restored, making Xi'an, a city of mountains and waters, more lush, green and charming.

渭河
Weihe River

成语"泾渭分明"，是指渭河水混，泾河水清，泾河的水流入渭河时，清浊不混，比喻界限清楚。

渭河横亘关中平原中部，自西向东，依序承接了涝河、沣河、灞河等南山一级支流，及至从高原南下的泾河汇入，缔造出"泾渭分明"的自然奇观和文化景观，众流滔滔，一路向东，汇入中华民族母亲河——黄河。

"秋风吹渭水，落叶满长安。"贾岛的诗句真切地道出了渭河是长安的水脉。汉、唐王朝定都长安，每年需通过渭河运输数百万石粮食到长安，渭河上粮船络绎不绝。

2019年，黄河流域生态保护和高质量发展上升为国家战略，为西安加强黄河最大支流——渭河水系的山水林田湖草人生命共同体的构建提供了根本遵循，也为做好新时代治水管水工作提供了科学指南。

闽国扬帆去，蟾蜍亏复圆。
秋风生渭水，落叶满长安。
——【唐】贾岛《忆江上吴处士》（节选）

● 泾渭分明
Distinct Water Colors at the Intersection of Jinghe and Weihe Rivers

The idiom "as different as the waters of the Jinghe and the Weihe" means that the Weihe River is muddy while the Jinghe River is clear. When the Jinghe River flows into the Weihe River, their water colors are entirely different, which means metaphorically that the boundary between two things is clear-cut.

The Weihe River runs across the central part of Guanzhong Plain from west to east, and successively receives the first-class tributaries of the southern mountains, such as the Laohe River, the Fenghe River, the Bahe River, etc., and finally merges with the Jinghe River flowing south from the plateau, creating a "distinct" natural spectacle and cultural landscape. All these waters continue to move east and empty into the Yellow River, the mother river of the Chinese nation.

"The autumn wind blew the Weihe River, and the fallen leaves flew over the capital of Chang'an." These lines written by Jia Dao clearly suggest that the Weihe River is the water vein of Chang'an. The capital of Han and Tang Dynasties was Chang'an, so millions of stones of grain must be transported to Chang'an every year via the Weihe River. There were numerous grain carriers on it.

In 2019, the ecological protection and high-quality development of the Yellow River Basin rose to be the national strategy, which has provided a fundamental principle for Xi'an to abide by in strengthening the construction of the life community of mountains, rivers, forests, lakes, grasslands and people in the Weihe River system, the largest tributary of the Yellow River, and also provided a scientific guide for doing a good job in water management in the new era.

泾河
Jinghe River

泾河是黄河支流渭河的第一大支流。泾河历史悠久，文化底蕴丰厚。泾河龙王、柳毅传说等故事流传久远。泾河流域是周人祖先生活的地方，周人在泾河流域发展了中国早期的农业。秦代著名的郑国渠、近代的泾惠渠等都是泾河重要的水利工程。

古人云泾河，水流本浑浊。

今我来泾州，见水绕城郭。

——【元】陈宜甫《泾河诗一首寄王克斋同知》（节选）

● 泾河
Jinghe River

The Jinghe River is the largest tributary of the Weihe River, which is also a tributary of the Yellow River. The Jinghe River has a long history and rich cultural heritage. Stories such as the Dragon King of the Jinghe River and the legend of Liu Yi have been circulating for a long time. The Jinghe River Basin is the place where the ancestors of the Zhou (dynasty) people lived and developed the early Chinese agriculture. The famous Zheng Guo Canal of Qin Dynasty and the Jinghui Canal of modern times are an important water conservancy Project on the Jinghe River.

沣河

　　沣河是黄河支流渭河的右岸支流，位于关中中部西安西南，与渭河平行东流，在草滩农场西汇入渭河。其流域内的沣惠渠，在沣河、潏河会合口下，从沣河东岸引水，是"关中八惠"渠之一。

　　沣河还是著名的文化之河。周代丰、镐两京即建在沣河东西两岸，沣河是周都镐京的主要水源，都城沿沣河而建；沣河是《诗经》的故乡，西汉的昆明池遗址在沣河东岸。

The Fenghe River is a tributary on the right bank of the Weihe River, a tributary of the Yellow River. Located in the southwest of Xi'an in the central part of Guanzhong, it flows east in parallel with the Weihe River, and merges into the Weihe River in the west of Caotan Farm. The Fenghui Canal in its basin, which draws water from the east bank of the Fenghe River below the confluence of the Fenghe River and the Juehe River, is one of the "Eight Irrigation Canals in Guanzhong".

The Fenghe River is also a famous river of culture. The capitals of Feng and Hao in Zhou Dynasty were respectively built on the east and west banks of the Fenghe River, which was the main water source of Capital of Hao in Zhou Dynastybuilt along the Fenghe River. The Fenghe River is the hometown of *The Book of Songs*, and Kunming Pond Site of Western Han Dynasty is on the east bank of the Fenghe River.

● 沣河
　Fenghe River

澇河，古称潦水，系古都长安八水之一。主要流域在西安市鄠邑区境内，发源于秦岭梁的静峪脑，源出涝峪，在三过村东北汇入渭河。

澇河，是"长安八水"中距西安城区最远的一条，也是"八水"中世人相对陌生的一条，但在历史文化方面，它有着自己独特的光彩。早在 6000 年前，即有先民在涝河流域繁衍生息。周文王姬昌在沣水西岸建立丰京后，为了保卫京城，计划在丰京西部建一"卫星"城，经过考察，认为"涝东有府地""涝西有福地"，于是在涝河东岸修筑了扈城。

The Laohe River, called Laoshui in ancient times, is one of the eight rivers in Chang'an, the ancient capital. Its main watershed is located in Huyi District, Xi'an. It originates from Jingyunao of Qinling mountain ridge, flows out of Laoyu Valley, and merges into the Weihe River in northeast of Sanguo Village.

The Laohe River is the farthest one from Xi'an city and also a relatively unfamiliar one among the "eight rivers around Chang'an", but it has its own unique brilliance in history and culture. As early as 6,000 years ago, ancestors flourished in the Laohe River Basin. After establishing Fengjing the capital on the west bank of the Fenghe River, King Wenwang of Zhou Dynasty, Ji Chang, planned to build a satellite city in the west of Fengjing in order to defend the capital. After investigation, it was considered that "there is a rich land on the east of the Laohe River" and "there is a blessed land on the west of the Laohe River". Therefore, the city Hu (today's Huyi District) was built on the east bank of the Laohe River.

一水喷珠从地起，千峰竞秀与天连。
澇水远从千涧合，终南直射百川回。
——【清】乔振翼《初夏观胡公泉》（节选）

澇河
Laohe River

潏河
Juehe River

来往城南十八年，赖家桥上潏河也。

——【唐】罗隐《下杜城》（节选）

潏河发源于长安区秦岭北坡的大峪，古称沇水，今亦称决河。出峪后，流经引镇、王莽街道等地，汇入沣河。潏河较大的支流有小峪河、太峪河、滈河、金沙河等，是长安城南的主要水系。

据宋代宋敏求《长安志》第十二卷记："潏水在县南一十里，东自万年县界流入。"初唐训诂学家颜师古对此处做了脚注："潏，音决。"

潏河流经因唐代诗人崔护的一首《题都城南庄》五言绝句而家喻户晓的桃溪堡村——"去年今日此门中，人面桃花相映红。人面不知何处去，桃花依旧笑春风。"

● 潏河
Juehe River

The Juehe River, called Jueshui in ancient times, originates from Dayu Valley on the northern slope of the Qinling Mountains in Chang'an District. After leaving the valley, it flows through Yinzhen Town, Wangmang Street and other places, and first merges into the Fenghe River. Its larger tributaries include such rivers as Xiaoyuhe, Taiyuhe, Haohe and Jinshahe. It is the main water system in the south of Chang'an City.

According to the twelfth volume of Song Minqiu's Annals of Chang'an in the Song Dynasty, "The Juehe River is ten li (about 5 kilometers) south of the county and flows in from Wannian County in the east." Yan Shigu, an annotator in the early Tang Dynasty, made a footnote here: "The name of the river is pronounced Jue".

The Juehe River passes through Taoxibao Village, which is well-known for its five-character quatrain titled "On the South Village of the Capital City" written by Tang Dynasty poet Cui Hu, which reads: "On this very day of last spring, close at the door, a young woman's face and peach blossoms set each other off. The maiden's face is nowhere to be found, while the peach blossoms remain smiling at the spring breeze. "

滈河 Haohe River

滈河，柳青的小说《创业史》中常常提到的"汤河"就是指的"滈河"，柳青就是在滈河之畔的皇甫村写就《创业史》这部长篇小说的。

滈河，《水经注》水道图中叫"交水"，《长安志》水道图中称"福水"，发源于西安市长安区石砭峪。与潏河在长安区郭杜街办香积寺汇合后向西，在鄠邑区秦渡镇附近注入沣河。

"Tanghe River", which is often mentioned in Liu Qing's novel Builders of a New Life, actually refers to "Haohe River". Liu Qing wrote this novel in Huangfu Village on the bank of the Haohe River.

The Haohe River is called "Jiaoshui" in the waterway map of Notes on Book of Water and "Fushui" in the waterway map of Annals of Chang'an. It originates from Shibianyu Valley in Chang'an District, Xi'an. It merges with the Juehe River near Xiangji Temple in Guodu Street Neighborhood, Chang'an District, and then flows west into the Fenghe River near Qindu Town, Huyi District.

三秋未获故人书，春到滈河忆旧居。
细雨槐香当日梦，满庭月色尚如初。
——冯其庸《终南山杂诗》

滈河 ▶
Haohe River

灞河
Bahe River

杨柳含烟灞岸春，年年攀折为行人。

好风若借低枝便，莫遣青丝扫路尘。

——【唐】李益《途中寄李二》

灞河有"玄灞"之称，指灞河水深且广，水色浑厚。灞河发源于秦岭北坡蓝田县灞源镇麻家坡以北。流经灞桥区、未央区，在西安市未央区、灞桥区之间汇入渭河。

灞河是渭河的主要支流，古名滋水，春秋时秦穆公称霸西戎后改名霸水。后来在"霸"字旁加上三点水，称为灞水。

有唐一代，沿岸遍植柳树、设置驿站，行旅者东向出行，长安亲友均在此折柳设宴送别。暮春之际，柳絮纷飞如雪，恰如离人的惆怅心绪，"年年柳色，灞陵伤别""羌笛何须怨杨柳，春风不度玉门关"，日月沉淀，情景交融，诗意盎然的"灞柳风雪"成为"关中八景"中的自然、文化双遗产。

The Bahe River is known as "Xuanba", which means that the Bahe River is deep, wide and rich in color. The Bahe River originates from the north of Majiapo in Bayuan Town, Lantian County on the northern slope of the Qinling Mountains. It flows through Baqiao District and Weiyang District, and joins the Weihe

River between the two districts of Xi 'an.

The Bahe River is the main tributary of the Weihe River, which was named Zishui in ancient times. In the Spring and Autumn Period, Duke Mugong of Qin State changed its name to Bashui, in which "Ba" originally means "hegemony", after he succeeded in dominating the western regions. Later, a component implying water was added next to the Chinese character "Ba", which is still used today.

In Tang Dynasty, willow trees were planted and courier stations were set up at intervals all along the river. When travelers headed eastward, their relatives and friends in Chang'an would prepare farewell banquets and sent them willow twigs as presents here. In the late spring, catkins were flying like snow, just like the melancholy mood of travellers. As some poetic lines put it, "Willow trees turn green every year, but travelers are saddened by their departures"; "Why play the sad song "Picking up a Willow Branch" with Qiang flute, when the spring breeze can't blow outside Yumen Pass?" In these poems, the sun and the moon make a contrast, and the scenes are blended together. The poetic picture of "willows and snow of the Bahe River" has become the only heritage of both nature and culture in the "Eight Attractions in Guanzhong".

灞河 ▼
Bahe River

浐河 Chanhe River

浐河素有"素浐"之称。"素浐"指浐河水清且浅。浐河是灞河的最大一级支流，发源于秦岭北麓的蓝田县西南汤峪镇。唐代诗人崔日用有诗句"东郊风物正熏馨，素浐凫鹥戏绿汀"。马戴《春日寻浐川王处士》一诗描写浐河景色"碧草径微断，白云扉晚开。罢琴松韵发，鉴水月光来。宿鸟排花动，樵童浇竹回。与君同露坐，涧石拂青苔。"

2019年，西安实施浐灞两岸点亮工程，打造夜景观光区，再现了"长安天街白如昼，璀璨星汉不夜城"的绚丽景象，展示大西安现代、时尚、绿色新形象。

The Chanhe River is known as "plain". "Plain" means that the river is clear and not deep. The Chanhe River, the largest tributary of the Bashe River, originates from Tangyu Town on the northern slope of the Qinling Mountains in the southwest of Lantian County. Cui Riyong, a poet in Tang Dynasty, once wrote a poem that reads, "The

青门烟野外，渡浐送行人。
鸭卧溪沙暖，鸠鸣社树春。
——【唐】温庭筠《早春浐水送友人》（节选）

scenery in the eastern suburb is fully fragrant, and waterfowls are playing on the green islets". Ma Dai's poem "Looking for Mr. Wang of the Bahe River in Spring" describes the scenery of the Chanhe River most vividly: "Thriving grasses nearly covers the narrow path in spring, and a recluse often opens his door late. The lyre being quiet, the soughing wind can be heard from the pines, while the moonlight comes out of the water as if from a mirror. The birds find their lodgings in the swarming flowers, and the woodman returns home after watering the bamboo. I sit with my dear friend and evening dews, while mosses are creeping onto the white stones."

In 2019, with the theme of "Fantastic Chan-Ba Rivers and A Charming New Year", through the lighting project on both sides of the two rivers, the night sightseeing area with the characteristics of the river represented the magnificent scene of "Chang'an Celestial Street being as bright as day, and night never falling with brilliant stars and lights so gay". Romantic elements are infused into the Chinese Year of Great Xi'an, thus to show the new image of the eastern part as a new center of Great Xi'an - modern, fashionable and international.

西安浐灞国家湿地公园鸟岛
Xi'an Chanba National Wetland Park—Bird Island

渼陂湖

Meibei Lake

万顷浸天色，千寻穷地根。
舟移城入树，岸阔水浮村。
闲鹭惊箫管，潜虬傍酒樽。
暝来呼小吏，列火俨归轩。

——【唐】岑参
《与鄠县群官宴渼陂》

杜甫曾与岑参兄弟同游渼陂湖胜景，并留下《渼陂行》的乐府诗。

渼陂，即渼水汇成之陂，一弘荡漾，也称美陂。其水甘美，陂中产鱼也甚美，位于西安市鄠邑区涝河西畔，有"关中山水最佳处"之美誉。是唐代游览胜地，湖区范围内有周季王陵、秦九女冢、空翠堂等景点遗迹十多处。苏轼、程颢等文人墨客也曾在此泛舟、赋诗。

涝河渼陂湖水系生态修复工程是陕西省坚持柔性治水理念，重点打造的关中水系三大湖池之一，是涝河蓄滞洪区建设的重点工程。

渼陂湖 ⬢
Meibei Lake

Du Fu once traveled with Cen Shen and his brother to enjoy the beautiful scenery of Meibei Lake, and left this ballad-styled poem "A Tour on Meibei Lake".

Meibei literally means a pond made by the Mei River. It is also called "pretty pond" due to the sparkling ripples on the surface of the lake. Its water is sweet and the fish in it can provide wonderful ingredients for palatable cuisine. Located on the west bank of the Laohe River in Huyi District, Xi'an, Meibei Lake boasts the fame of having "the best landscape in Guanzhong". It was a imperial garden in a resort in Tang Dynasty. There are more than ten scenic spots and historical remains in the lake area, such as Mausoleum of King Jiwang of Zhou Dynasty, Nine Daughters' Tomb of Qin Dynasty and Kongcui Hall. Su Shi, Cheng Hao and other scholars once rowed boats and wrote poems here.

The ecological restoration project of Meibei Lake system of the Laohe River is one of the key projects to build three great lakes or ponds in Guanzhong River system in Shaanxi Province by abiding by the flexible water conservancy principle. And it is also the key project in the construction of flood storage and detention area on the Laohe River.

昆明池，位于陕西省西安市长安区鱼斗路，地处西安城西的沣水、潏水之间。昆明池总面积3.32平方千米。

汉武帝元狩三年（前120），武帝为征讨西南，拓宽西周丰镐"灵沼"水地，以象滇池，从而训练大汉水师，因此开凿昆明池。

昆明池作为中国古代较大的人工湖，开大型水体为核心的园林建设的先河，还有三大作用：一是昆明池可以为渠运提供水源和皇室游幸，二是重要的水产养殖基地，三是关中大运河漕渠的主要水源。

昆明池东岸有牵牛石像，池西岸有织女石像，由火成岩雕成，造型古朴、粗犷。后人将这双石像分别称为石婆、石父，是我国现存较早的大型石雕作品之一。汉武帝时雕刻的两条石鲸之一原立于汉昆明池遗址边，据《三辅故事》载，此石鲸"长三丈，每至雷雨，常鸣吼，鬐尾皆动"。

春豫灵池会，沧波帐殿开。
舟凌石鲸度，槎拂斗牛回。
——【唐】宋之问
《奉和晦日幸昆明池应制》（节选）

● 昆明池
Kunming Pond

Kunming Pool is located at Yudou Road in Chang'an District, Xi'an, Shaanxi Province, between the Fenghe River and the Juehe River in the west of Xi'an City. The total area of Kunming Pond is 3.32 square kilometers.

In the third year (120 B.C.) of Emperor Wudi of Han Dynasty, in order to go on a punitive expedition to the southwest, he expanded the "Lingzhao" water field in Feng and Hao of Western Zhou Dynasty to resemble Dianchi Lake in Kunming, Yunnan Province to train his navy, so he ordered to dig this Kunming Pond.

Kunming Pond, as a large artificial lake in ancient China, is the first garden construction project with large water body as the core, and has three major functions: first, providing a water source for canal transportation and a place for the royal family's amusement; second, acting as an important aquaculture base; and third, being a major water for the Grand Canal of Guanzhong .

There is a statue of the Cowherd on the east bank and a statue of Weaver Maid on the west bank of Kunming Pond, which are carved from igneous rock, and their shapes are unsophiscated and rugged. Later generations called this pair of stone statues Shipo (stone mother) and Shifu (stone father) respectively, which are two earliest existing large-scale stone carving works in China. One of the two stone whales carved during Emperor Wudi's reign in Han Dynasty originally stood by the Kunming Pond Site. The stone whale in Kunming Pond originally stood at the edge of Kunming Pond Site in Han Dynasty. According to Stories of Three Officials, this stone whale was "ten meters long, always roaring and moving in every thunderstorm".

　　汉城湖位于西安市西北，原为团结水库（古漕运明渠），由西库、中库、东库及团结库四个水库组成，据史料记载，汉代这里是长安城的漕运河道。如今，在汉城湖景区内立有汉武帝雕像一座，这是目前中国皇帝雕像中最大的一座——高21.5米，寓意着西汉统治215年。

　　与汉城湖毗邻的玉丰村是"朝衣东市"典故的发生地。西汉景帝时期，以吴王刘濞为首发动的"七国之乱"声势浩大，汉景帝无力抵抗，只有杀当时谏言削藩的晁错以缓解局势。晁错当天穿着皇帝赐给他的朝服，在汉长安城的东市被斩。

Hancheng Lake, located in the northwest of Xi'an, Shaanxi Province, was originally Tuanjie Reservoir (an open channel in ancient times), which consists of four parts - the west, the middle, the east and Tuanjie. In Han

Dynasty this was a waterway for transporting grain to the capital of Chang'an. At present, there is a statue of Emperor Wudi of Han Dynasty set up in Hancheng Lake Scenic Area, the largest statue of Chinese emperors so far - 21.5 meters high, which symbolizes the 215-year rule of the Western Han Dynasty.

Yufeng Village, adjacent to Hancheng Lake, is the place where a touching story happened. During the reign of Emperor Jingdi of Western Han Dynasty, the "Rebellion of the Seven Kingdoms" initiated by King Liu Bi of Wu, was so violent and strong that Emperor Jingdi could not resist it. So the emperor had to execute Chao Cuo, the fervent advocate for abolishing separatist rules in all the kingdoms, to alleviate the grave situation. On the same day, Chao Cuo, wearing the court dress given to him by the emperor, was beheaded in the East Marketof Chang'an.

"三月三日天气新，长安水边多丽人。"曲江池曾经是我国汉唐时期一处极为富丽优美的园林。每到春秋两分及重要节日，城里的皇室贵族、达官显贵都会携家眷来此游赏，樽壶酒浆，笙歌画船，宴乐于曲江水上，新科进士及第也要在曲江赐宴。新科进士在这里乘兴作乐，放杯至盘上，放盘于曲流上，盘随水转，轻漂漫泛，转至谁前，谁就执杯畅饮，遂成一时盛事。"曲江流饮"由此得名。据《全唐诗》记载，大诗人李白、杜甫、白居易、李商隐、张籍、元稹、刘禹锡、韦应物、温庭筠、卢照邻等都曾到曲江一游，给世人留下许多脍炙人口的优美诗句。

"On the third day of the third lunar month, in the freshening weather, more beauties can be seen by the waterside in Chang'an." Qujiang Pond was once a very rich and beautiful garden in Han and

一片花飞减却春，风飘万点正愁人。

且看欲尽花经眼，莫厌伤多酒入唇。

——【唐】杜甫《曲江二首（其一）》（节选）

Tang Dynasties in China. Every spring and autumn equinox and important festivals, the royal families, dignitaries and officials in the city would come here to enjoy themselves with vintage wine, singing and dancing, dining and partying in gaily painted pleasure boats on Qujiang Pond. Scholars who had just won higher titles in the imperial examinations would arrange a banquet, too. They would take this opportunity to make fun by placing a cup on a plate and then floating the plate on the meander. The plate turned with the currents and floated lightly on the surface. Whoever got the turning plate close at hand would hold up the cup and drink the wine in it - a grand event indeed! Hence it got the term "drinking along with the flowing water of Qujiang Pond". According to Complete Poetry of Tang Dynasty, great poets like Li Bai, Du Fu, Bai Juyi, Li Shangyin, Zhang Ji, Yuan Zhen, Liu Yuxi, Wei Yingwu, Wen Tingyun and Lu Zhaolin all visited Qujiang, leaving the world with many beautiful poems.

今曲江池夜景 ▼
Night Scene of Qujiang Pond

秦岭四宝享盛名

Four Treasures of Qinling Mountains in High Repute

　　秦岭动植物资源丰富，原始生态保存完好。大熊猫、金丝猴、羚牛、朱鹮更被誉为"秦岭四宝"。以它们为原型设计的熊熊、金金、羚羚、朱朱是中华人民共和国第十四届运动会的吉祥物。2021 年 5 月 28 日，为打响秦岭大熊猫文化品牌建造的秦岭四宝科学公园正式开园，成为保护秦岭自然生态和发展文旅产业的新亮点。

The Qinling Mountains is rich in animal and plant resources, and its original ecology is well preserved. Giant pandas, golden monkeys, takins and crested ibis are also known as the "Four Treasures of Qinling Mountains". Xiong Xiong, Jin Jin, Ling Ling, and Zhu Zhu, which are designed with these animals as prototypes, are the mascots of the 14th Games of the People's Republic of China. On May 28, 2021, the Qinling Four Treasures Science Park, which had been built to launch the brand of giant panda culture in the Qinling Mountains, officially opened, which became a new highlight in protecting the natural ecology of the Qinling Mountains and developing the cultural tourism industry.

秦岭四宝科学动物园 ●
The Qinling Four Treasures
Science Park

朱鹮
Crested Ibis

　　朱鹮素有鸟中"东方宝石"之称。古称朱鹭、红朱鹭。曾广泛分布于中国东部、日本、俄罗斯、朝鲜等地，由于环境恶化等因素导致种群数量急剧下降，至 20 世纪 80 年代仅中国陕西省洋县秦岭南麓有 7 只野生种群，后经人工繁殖，种群数量已达到 3000 只。

　　中国古代，人们认为朱鹮能带来吉祥，把朱鹮作为"吉祥之鸟"，朱鹮更被日本皇室视为圣鸟。朱鹮的拉丁学名"Nipponia Nippon"直译为"日本的日本"，以国名命名鸟名，足见朱鹮对于日本的重要性。

　　朱鹮栖息于海拔 1200~1400 米的疏林地带，在附近的溪流、沼泽及稻田内涉水，漫步觅食小鱼、蟹、蛙、螺等水生动物，兼食昆虫；在高大的树木上休息及夜宿；每年繁殖一窝，每窝产卵 2~4 枚，由双亲孵化及育雏，孵化期约 30 天，性成熟为 3 岁，寿命最长纪录为 37 年。

　　截至 2021 年，朱鹮在全球有 5000 多只，中国境内有约 4400 只，陕西有约 4100 只，分布在陕西汉中市洋县、城固县，安康市宁陕县等地。

朱鹮 ⬮
Crested Ibis

Crested ibis is known as the "oriental gem" among birds. In ancient times, it was called heron or red heron. It had been widely distributed in eastern China, Japan, Russia, Korea and other places, but its population decreased sharply due to environmental degradation and other factors. By 1980s, there were 7 wild ibises discovered at the southern foot of the Qinling Mountains in Yangxian County, Shaanxi Province, China, and after artificial propagation, its population reached 3,000.

In ancient China, people thought that crested ibis could bring good fortune, and regarded it as an "auspicious bird". Crested ibis was regarded as a holy bird by the Japanese royal family. Its Latin name "Nipponia Nippon" can be literally translated as "Japan's Japan". The fact that the bird is named after a country shows how significant it is to Japan.

Crested ibis inhabits the sparse forest zone at an altitude of 1200~1400 meters, wading in nearby streams, swamps and rice fields, strolling for aquatic animals such as small fish, crabs, frogs and snails to eat, and feeding on insects too. It rests and stays overnight on tall trees. Each year, one brood is bred, and 2~4 eggs are laid in each brood. The incubation period is about 30 days, the sexual maturity is 3 years, and the longest life record is 37 years.

Up to 2021, there are more than 5,000 crested ibises in the world, Among them, about 4,400 crested ibises are in China while as many as about 4,100 crested ibises live in Shaanxi, which are distributed in Yangxian County and Chenggu County of Hanzhong, and Ningshan County of Ankang, Shaanxi.

外界印象大熊猫只生活在四川一带，实际上陕西秦岭也有大熊猫。四川大熊猫，头比较大，头型偏长，长得更像熊；而陕西秦岭大熊猫，头圆嘴短，长得更像猫。

研究表明，两地熊猫虽然同宗同源，但受到嘉陵江阻隔、人类活动的影响，数万年前，它们就断绝了往来，无法联姻，开始各自独立繁衍、进化的过程。

根据新的动物分类学研究结果，将大熊猫分为四川亚种和秦岭亚种，秦岭亚种仅占 18.5%。它比其他五大山系的大熊猫更为原始，种群数量更少，栖息地更狭窄，生存情况更为濒危。陕西汉中大熊猫自然保护区又称佛坪自然保护区位于秦岭中段南坡，是以保护大熊猫为主的森林和野生动物类型的自然保护区，总面积 29240 公顷。本区大熊猫毛色奇特，不但有黑白色大熊猫，而且多次发现棕白色和白色大熊猫。

碧峰峡熊猫基地的大熊猫
Giant Pandas in Bifengxia Panda Base

The external impression is that giant pandas only grow in Sichuan. In fact, there are giant pandas in the Qinling Mountains of Shaanxi Province. Sichuan giant panda has a big, long-shaped head and looks more like a bear while the giant panda in the Qinling Mountains, Shaanxi Province, has a round head and short mouth and looks more like a cat.

Studies have shown that although the pandas in the two places belong to the same family with the same origin, they were cut off from each other many years ago due to the barrier of the Jialing River and the influence of human activities. They were unable to get united with intermarriage, so they began the process of independent reproduction and evolution.

According to the new results of animal taxonomy, giant pandas are divided into Sichuan subspecies and Qinling subspecies, with Qinling subspecies accounting for only 18.5%. The Qinling panda is more primitive than the giant pandas in the other five mountain ranges, with smaller numbers, narrower habitats and more endangered living conditions. Shaanxi Hanzhong Giant Panda Nature Reserve, also known as Foping Nature Reserve, is located on the southern slope of the middle part of the Qinling Mountains. It is a forest and wildlife type nature reserve with a total area of 29,240 hectares. Giant pandas in this area have peculiar fur color. Not only black and white pandas, but also brown and white pandas have been found many times.

◀

大熊猫
Giant Panda

羚牛 Takin

秦岭羚牛，又被称为"秦岭金毛扭角羚"，当地人又叫它为"白羊"或是"羊子"，体形粗大，肩高 100~130 厘米，尾长 15~20 厘米，重量 250~400 千克。雄性和雌性均具较短的角，是一种大型牛科食草动物。两个长而粗壮的前肢，两条短而弯曲的后腿，以及分叉的偶蹄，这些特点都使秦岭羚牛能够适应高山攀爬生活。

秦岭羚牛在每年的二月前后产崽，每胎一崽。它们生性警觉，听觉灵敏。通常是少则十几头，多则四五十头组成羚牛群一起生活。

秦岭羚牛属国家一级保护动物。数量非常稀少，在世量不足 5000 头。

Qinling takin, also known as "Qinling golden yakin", is also called "white sheep" or "sheep" by locals. It has a large body shape and a shoulder height of 100-130cm; the tail length is 15-20cm; and the weight is 250-400kg. Both male and female have short horns, and they are large herbivores of cattle family. Its two long and stout forelimbs, two short and curved hind legs and forked cloven hoofs enable Qinling takins to adapt better to the life of climbing mountains.

Qinling takins give birth around February every year, one cub for each. They are alert by nature and have a keen sense of hearing. Usually, as few as a dozen takins or as many as forty or fifty takins flock together.

Qinling takin is a national first-class protected animal. The number is very rare, with less than 5,000 in the world.

羚牛 ●
Takin

金丝猴

Golden Monkey

　　秦岭金丝猴，在动物学分类上属四川金丝猴的秦岭种群。

　　它体长 57~76 厘米，尾长 51~72 厘米，雄性体重 15~39 千克，雌性体重 6.5~7.0 千克。鼻孔向上仰，颜面部为蓝色，无颊囊。

　　秦岭是中国金丝猴分布的最北限，金丝猴大多活动在 2000~3000 米的高海拔山区的针阔混交林地带，过着群居生活，以野果、嫩枝芽、树叶为食。

　　秦岭金丝猴主要分布于陕西境内秦岭山区的周至、太白、宁陕、佛坪、洋县等地。据调查，野生秦岭金丝猴约有 3000~5000 只。

Qinling golden monkey belongs to Qinling subcategory of Sichuan golden monkey in zoological taxonomy.

It has a body length of 57-76cm, a tail length of 51-72cm, a male weight of 15-39kg and a female weight of 6.5 -7.0kg, with nose upturned, face blue and no cheek pouch.

The Qinling Mountains is the northernmost limit of the distribution of golden monkeys in China. Most of the golden monkeys live in the mixed coniferous and broad-leaved forest zone in the high-altitude mountain area of 2000-3000 meters, living in groups and feeding on wild fruits, shoots and leaves.

Golden monkeys in the Qinling Mountains are mainly distributed in Zhouzhi, Taibai, Ningshan, Foping and Yangxian counties in Shaanxi Province. According to the survey, there are about 3000-5000 golden monkeys in the Qinling Mountains.

蓝田日暖半坡前
Charm of Primitive Human Sites in Lantian and Banpo

　　涓滴之水起自秦岭之巅，跳跃跌宕，入渭归黄，东流进海，勾勒出一条中华文化的发展轴。山水形胜滋养了华夏祖脉，中华民族自此发祥，炎黄印记在此镌刻，中国文化缘此勃兴，接力有序，勇立潮头，共同演绎出中华传统文化迭代跃迁的宏大交响。

　　A trickle of water starts from the top of the Qinling Mountains, jumps up and down, flows into the Weihe River and then into the Yellow River, and finally empties into the sea in the east, draw the outline of a development axis of Chinese civilization. The beauty of the mountains and rivers nourishes the ancestral veins of China, and the Chinese nation has been born here since then. The marks of the Chinese ancestors, Emperor Yandi and the Yellow Emperor have been engraved here on this land. The Chinese culture therefore thrives here, is relayed successively, forges ahead courageously, and has jointly rendered the grand symphony of iterative progress of the Chinese traditional culture.

山水相偎相依，人类休戚与共。旧石器时代距今 212 万年前，逐灞河上游、依秦岭北麓而居的古人类，在蓝田县玉山镇上陈村留下目前已知西安地区最早的人类遗迹。距今 115 万年前，目前已知亚洲北部最古老的直立人——蓝田猿人出现于隔河相望的玉山镇公王岭。

蓝田人于 1963 年被发现，化石为一个三十多岁女性的头骨。第二年 5 月，又在公王岭地层中发现一个基本保存完整的中年女性头骨化石，后复原出一完整的猿人头骨。蓝田人的生活年代，本来认为是距今约 69 万年到 95 万年，但是 1987 年重新测定后认为是距今约 70 万年到 115 万年。

蓝田人的发现扩大了我国猿人的分布范围，丰富了人类物质文化纪录，它的发现把人类活动的时间上溯了五六十万年，填补了人类进化史上的一个缺环，为研究人类起源提供了珍贵的科学资料。

四面八方的游客来到公王岭，与远古的祖先在宇宙中对话，若想了解从狩猎采集、茹毛饮血到今日拥有高度发达文明的人类的发展历程，一定要去玉山公王岭蓝田猿人遗址博物馆走一走，追寻远古的祖先披荆斩棘、风雨凄迷的生活。

● 蓝田猿人遗址
Lantian Ape-man Site

Mountains and rivers depend on each other, and human beings share their weal and woe. In the Paleolithic Age, 2.12 million years ago, ancient humans who lived along the upper reaches of the Bahe River and the northern foot of the Qinling Mountains left the earliest human remains in Xi'an at Shangchen Village in Yushan Town, Lantian County. About 1.15 million years ago, Lantian Ape Man, the oldest Homo erectus in northern Asia, appeared in Gongwangling, Yushan Town across the river.

Lantian Ape Man was discovered in 1963. The fossil is the skull of a woman in her thirties. In May of the following year, a well-preserved middle-aged female skull fossil was found in Gongwangling formation. A complete ape-man skull fossil was recovered later. The life time of Lantian Ape Man was originally thought to be about 690,000 to 950,000 years ago, but after re-measurement in 1987, it was thought to be about 700,000 to 1.15 million years ago.

The discovery of Lantian Ape Man has expanded the distribution range of ape men in China and enriched the material and cultural records of human beings. Its discovery has traced the time of human activities back to 500,000 to 600,000 years, filled a gap in the history of human evolution, and provided precious scientific data for studying the origin of human beings.

Tourists from all directions come to Gongwangling to have a dialogue with the ancient ancestors across the universe. If you want to know the development process of human beings from hunting and gathering to having highly developed civilization today, you must go to the Lantian Ape-man Site Museum in Gongwangling at Mount Yushan, and search for the traces of the formidable yet vigorous life of the ancient ancestors.

6000 年前，新石器时代中期半坡人在浐河之滨缔造了令人叹为观止的仰韶文化典型。半坡遗址是有 6000~6700 多年历史的新石器时代仰韶文化聚落遗址，对聚落形态和中国原始社会历史研究有着重要的科学价值。其位于西安市浐河东岸，遗址占地面积约 5 万平方米。其上建有中华人民共和国第一座史前聚落遗址博物馆——西安半坡博物馆。

半坡遗址分为居住区、墓葬区和制陶作坊区。从出土的石斧、石锛、石铲、石刀、石碾等生产工具和陶罐、陶盆、小口尖底瓶等生活用具来看，半坡人过着以农业为主，渔猎为辅的生活。在一些陶钵的口沿上还刻有各种符号，有 20~30 种之多，这些符号可能是中国文字的起源。

About 6000 years ago, Banpo people in the middle of Neolithic Age created an amazing Yangshao culture model on the banks of the Chanhe River. Banpo Village is a settlement site of Yangshao culture in Neolithic Age with a history of more than 6000~6700 years, and has important scientific value for the study of settlement form and Chinese primitive social history. It is located on the east bank of the Chanhe River in Xi'an, and the site covers an area of about 50,000 square meters. On it is built the first prehistoric settlement site museum of the People's Republic of China - Xi'an Banpo Museum.

Banpo Site is divided into residential area, burial area and pottery workshop area. Judging from the unearthed production tools such as stone axe, stone shovel, stone knife and stone mill, as well as living utensils such as pottery pots, pottery basins and bottles with small mouth and pointed bottom, Banpo people lived a life with agriculture as the mainstay, supplemented by fishing and hunting. There are 20~30 kinds of symbols engraved on the edges of some pottery pots, which may be the origin of Chinese characters.

西安半坡博物馆
Banpo Museum

千年古都　盛世华章

西安　卷二

CHAPTER TWO SPLENDID LEGACIES OF THE
ANCIENT CAPITAL OF A MILLENNIUM

大雁塔及玄奘雕像
Dayan Pagoda and statue of XuanZang

● 大雁塔灯光秀
Dayan Pagoda Light Show

长安，自古被称为"神州龙首""中原脊梁"，是"世界四大文明古都"之一。七千年文明史层累，十三朝古都代际叠加，融中汇西、多元包容，创造出灿烂辉煌的物质文化遗产、非物质文化遗产。现拥有秦始皇帝陵及兵马俑坑、汉长安城未央宫遗址、唐长安城大明宫遗址、大雁塔、小雁塔、兴教寺塔等 6 处世界文化遗产。

中国历史上，曾有西周、秦、西汉、新、东汉、西晋、前赵、前秦、后秦、西魏、北周、隋、唐共 13 个王朝在西安建都。

西安是一座具有光荣革命传统的城市，红色资源十分丰富，发生过许多可歌可泣的革命故事，拥有包括葛牌镇红二十五军军部旧址、西安事变旧址、西安八路军办事处等在内的127处珍贵的革命旧址（遗址），他们与诗词歌赋、翰墨丹青一起，记录着中华民族的薪火相传。

Xi'an, called Chang'an in history, has been named as "Dragon Head of the Divine Land" and "Backbone of the Central Plains" since ancient times, and it is one of the "four ancient capitals of civilization in the world". Its history of civilization has been accumulated for 7,000 years, and its status as the capital of thirteen dynasties overlaps from generation to generation, bringing together cultures from all around the world in a pluralistic and inclusive manner, and creating huge numbers of splendid tangible and intangible cultural heritages. At present, there are six world cultural heritages, including Qin Shihuang's Mausoleum and Terracotta Warriors and Horses, Weiyang Palace Site of Han Dynasty, Daming Palace Site of Tang Dynasty, Big Wild Goose Pagoda, Smalle Wild Goose Pagoda and Xingjiao Temple Pagoda.

In Chinese history, 13 dynasties, including Western Zhou Dynasty, Qin Dynasty, Western Han Dynasty, New Dynasty, Eastern Han Dynasty, Western Jin Dynasty, Former Zhao Dynasty, Former Qin Dynasty, Later Qin Dynasty, Western Wei Dynasty, Northern Zhou Dynasty, Sui Dynasty and Tang Dynasty, established their capital in Xi'an. Bronze wares of Zhou Dynasty, terracotta figures of Qin Dynasty, tomb mounds of Han Dynasty and Pagodas of Tang Dynasty remain appealing to the world even after so many years of changes.

Xi'an is a city with glorious revolutionary tradition, rich in red resources. Many heroic and touching revolutionary stories have happened here. There are 127 precious revolutionary sites (ruins) including the former site of Red 25th Army in Gepai Town, the former site of Xi'an Incident, the Eighth Route Army Xi'an Office, etc. Together with poems, songs, calligraphy works and paintings, they record the glory of the Chinese nation from generation to generation.

礼乐宗周何处寻
A Place to Enjoy the Rites and Music of Zhou Dynasty

　　赫赫宗周，寻梦周公。在西安市西南的沣河西岸和东岸分别坐落着周文王建立的"丰邑"和周武王建立的"镐京"，这是西周王朝的都城丰镐，也是长安作为国家都城出现的开始。

　　周公制礼作乐，确立礼乐制度，奠定了中国传统文化的基调，对中国文化产生了巨大而深远的影响。

Glory belongs to Zhou Dynasty, and the dream of nationhood originates from the Duke of Zhou (Zhougong). On the west bank and east bank of the Fenghe River, southwest of Xi 'an City are Fengyi established by King Wenwang and Haojing established by King Wuwang of Zhou Dynasty, which are collectively called "Fenghao", the capital of Western Zhou Dynasty. It is also the beginning of Chang'an's emergence as the national capital.

The Duke of Zhou established the Rites of Zhou and created the Classic of Music, setting up various institutions and systems, which set the tone for the Chinese traditional culture and had a great and far-reaching impact on the Chinese culture.

西周车马坑遗址
Chariot Burial Site of Western Zhou Dynasty

丰镐是中国历史上第一座规模宏大、布局整齐的都城。丰镐双子王城开启了中国的建城史、建都史，启碇了秩序森严的"方九里，旁三门""左祖右社，前朝后市"的城市空间营造法式。从西周丰镐开始，西安拉开了漫长而辉煌的建都史序幕。

　　周文王从"周原膴膴，堇荼如饴"的宝鸡地区迁都丰京，并灭掉了今西安市长安区沣河一带的崇国，"三分天下有其二"，继承文王剪商遗志的武王伐纣克殷，从而建立西周王朝。丰镐作为首都约是公元前 11 世纪中叶至公元前 771 年，经历了 11 代12 位周王。成康之治、昭王南征、穆王西游、国人暴动与宣王中兴的西周传奇在这里落英缤纷。丰镐遗址总面积约 17 平方千米，是全国重点文物保护单位。

周虽旧邦，其命维新。

——《诗经·大雅·文王》

Fenghao is the first capital city with large scale and neat layout in the Chinese history. The twin cities of Fenggao opened up the history of building cities and capitals in China, and initiated the orderly urban space construction method of "nine square li in area with three doors on each of the four sides" and "ancestral temple on the left and altar of land and grain on the right, in the front and marketplace in the back". Starting from Fenghao in Western Zhou Dynasty, Xi'an kicked off a long and glorious history of capital building.

King Wenwang moved his capital to Fengjing from Baoji area, where "the plain is very fertile, and the plants taste really sweet", and conquered Chong State in Fenghe (river) area in today's Chang'an District, Xi'an. "Possessing two thirds of the world" and carrying on his father King Wenwang's work, King Wuwang waged a war on Shang Dynasty, captured its capital of Yin, and subsequently established Western Zhou Dynasty. Fenghao was the capital from the middle of the 11th century B.C. to 771 B.C., and experienced 11 generations of 12 Zhou kings. Such legendary events as the Prosperity of Kings Chengwang and Kangwang, King Zhaowang's Southern Expedition, King Muwang's Western Tour, Freemen Uprising and King Xuanwang's Resurgence were all staged here. Fenghao Site, with a total area of about 17 square kilometers, is a national key cultural relic protection unit.

秦王虎视何雄哉
Emperor Qin Shihuang: A Ruler with
Great Talent and Bold Vision

　　秦朝是中国历史上第一个大一统王朝，秦始皇被视为千古一帝，秦文化以雄浑、慷慨而闻名于世。秦筑咸阳宫，以秦岭为城垣，以渭水为银汉，以终南为门阙，以四海归一、前无古人的宏大雄姿，开创了法天象地的都城建设格局。

● 秦始皇帝陵博物馆一号坑
Emperor Qin Shihuang's Mausoleum from Pit No.1

Qin Dynasty is the first unified country in the Chinese history. Emperor Qin Shihuang, literally the first emperor of Qin, is regarded as an outstanding emperor of the millennium, and Qin culture is famous for its boldness and generosity. Qin Dynasty built the grandest ever Xianyang Palace, imaginatively using the Qinling Mountains as the city wall, the Weihe River as the Milky Way on earth, and Mount Zhongnan as the gate. Having united all the states in China as one, it created the Costruction pattern of the capital construction with unprecedented grandeur.

秦始皇帝陵博物院位于距西安 37 千米的临潼区东，是以秦始皇兵马俑为基础、以秦始皇陵为依托的一座大型遗址博物院。秦兵马俑开创了中国等比真人、高度写实雕塑的先河，是古典中国塑造艺术臻于成熟的重要标志，被誉为"世界第八大奇迹"，先后有 200 余位外国元首慕名参观，其中部分文物多次代表中国出访巡展世界。

秦始皇兵马俑陪葬坑坐西向东，三坑呈"品"字形排列。一号俑坑左右两侧各有一个兵马俑坑，分别是二号坑和三号坑。一号坑兵俑列位整齐，具有典型的方阵特征，是列阵守卫的经典队形。二号坑内是一号坑的后援部队，三号坑是统率一、二号坑的指挥部。兵马俑群是秦军队"虎贲之士百余万，车千乘，骑万匹"的真实缩影，也是中国出现最早、规模最大的写实群雕。

"岂曰无衣，与子同袍，王于兴师，修我戈矛。"秦人一路东进，浩荡的秦风在这里生动而昂扬。

秦王扫六合，虎视何雄哉？

——【唐】李白《古风五十九首（其三）》（节选）

跪射俑
Kneeling Archer

将军俑
General

Qin Shihuang's Mausoleum Museum is located 37 kilometers east of Lintong District, Xi'an. It is a large-scale ruins museum based on Terracotta Warriors and Horses of Qin Shihuang and is supported by Qin Shihuang's Mausoleum. The Terracotta Warriors and Horses have created a precedent for Chinese sculpture which is equal to real people and highly realistic. It is an important symbol of the maturity of classical Chinese sculptural art, and is known as "the eighth wonder of the world". More than 200 foreign heads of state have visited the museum, and some cultural relics on behalf of China have been exhibited in other countries many times.

The burial pits of Terracotta Warriors and Horses of Qin Shihuang sit from west to east, and the three pits are arranged in the shape of a Chinese character " 品 ".

On the left and right sides of No.1 terracotta warriors pit are Pit No.2 and Pit No.3. The warriors in Pit No.1 are arranged neatly, with typical phalanx characteristics, and are in the classic formation of array guards. Pit No.2 is the backup force of Pit No.1, and pit No.3 is the headquarters commanding pits No. 1 and No. 2. The terracotta warriors and horses are the true epitome of the Qin army's "over one million warriors, a thousand chariots and ten thousand horses", and they are also the earliest and largest realistic group sculptures in China.

"Who says we have no robe to wear? Wear that robe with you. The king will send troops to fight, so I will trim my dagger and spear." The Qin soldiers marched eastward with high morale, and their fighting spirit soared aloft here.

秦始皇帝陵
Qin Shihuang's Mausoleum

秦铜车马是国宝级文物，是 20 世纪考古史上发现的结构最为复杂、形体最为庞大的古代青铜器，被誉为"青铜之冠"。

20 世纪 80 年代秦始皇帝陵封土西侧陪葬坑出土两乘大型陪葬铜车马，一前一后排列。经复原，大小约为真人真马的二分之一。制作年代不晚于公元前 210 年。铜车马主体为青铜所铸，一些零部件为金银饰品，秦代工匠成功地运用了铸造、焊接、镶嵌等工艺技术，并将其完美地结合为一个整体。

2021 年，"秦陵彩绘铜车马二号车"迁往新落成的秦始皇陵铜车马博物馆。该馆于 2021 年 5 月 18 日国际博物馆日试开放。

又有戎立车以征伐。

——【东汉】蔡邕《独断》（节选）

秦陵西侧陪葬坑出土的铜车马 ▼
Bronze chariots and horses unearthed from Burial pit on the west side of Qinling Mausoleum

Bronze chariots and horses of Qin are national treasures. They are ancient bronze wares with the most complex structure and the largest size discovered in the 20th century archaeological history, and are known as the "crown of bronze".

In 1980s, two sets of large bronze chariots and horses were unearthed from the burial pit on the west side of Qin Shihuang's Mausoleum, arranged in tandem. After restoration, they are about half the size of real people and horses. They were made before 210 B.C. The main body of bronze chariots and horses is made of bronze, and some parts are made of gold and silver as ornaments. Craftsmen in Qin Dynasty successfully applied various techniques such as casting, welding, inlaying and integrated them into a whole.

In 2021, "No. 2 painted bronze chariot and horses" was moved to the newly completed Bronze Chariots and Horses Museum located on the southwest of the grave mound in Lishan Garden. The museum opened on May 18, 2021, the International Museum Day.

秦始皇帝陵铜车马博物馆
The Museum of Bronze Chariot and Horses

滔滔热血汉衣冠
Han Dynasty: Decisive Period for the Chinese Culture

大汉王朝是中华文明重要的形成期，"布衣将相""浪漫奔放"的汉帝国如旭日朝阳，在长安磅礴而出。

Han Dynasty is an important formation period of the Chinese civilization, and the Han Empire, which is characterized by having "ministers and generals from among commoners" and being "romantic and unrestrained", emerged in Chang'an like the rising sun.

● 汉长安城东南角遗址
Site of Southeast Corner of Chang'an City in Han Dynasty

"长安"作为都城之名始于西汉，汉高祖七年（前200），刘邦采纳娄敬（刘敬）建议，将都城迁至"金城千里，天府之国"的关中，于渭河南岸、龙首原之北秦都咸阳的旧址建立大汉帝国的新首都，并定都城名称为"长安"，以祈望王朝"长治久安"。这就是赫赫有名的汉长安城，由此开启了西汉王朝长达 200 余年的统治。

汉长安城遗址位于今西安市未央区境内，西为皂河，东为汉城湖，历经 2200 多年整体格局完整保存至今，是中国现存规模宏大、遗迹丰富、格局明确、保存较为完整的古代统一帝国的都城遗址。

金城千里，天府之国。
——【汉】张良《史记·留侯列传》

Chang'an as the name of a capital city began in Western Han Dynasty. In the seventh year of Emperor Gaozu (200 B.C.), Liu Bang, adopted the suggestion made by Lou Jing (also called Liu Jing), moved the capital city to Guanzhong, where there was "a city of vast expanse, a land of abundance", and established the new capital of Great Han Empire at the former site of the Capital of Xianyang of Qin Dynasty on the south bank of the Weihe River and on the north of Longshouyuan. This is the famous Chang'an City of Han Dynasty, which started the rule of Western Han Dynasty for more than 200 years.

Chang'an City Site of Han Dynasty is located in today's Weiyang District, Xi'an City, with the Zaohe River in the west and Hancheng Lake in the east. After more than 2,200 years, its overall pattern has been preserved completely up to now, and it is the existing capital site of an ancient unified empire with large scale, rich relics, clear pattern and relatively complete preservation.

未央宫 Weiyang Palace

　　未央宫是西汉帝国的大朝正宫，政治中心和国家象征。建于汉高祖七年（前200），由重臣萧何监造，位于汉长安城地势最高的西南角龙首原上，又称西宫。自未央宫建成之后，西汉皇帝都居住在这里，成为汉帝国200余年间的政令中心，所以在后世的诗词中，未央宫成为汉宫的代名词。

　　未央宫是丝绸之路的东方起点，总面积有北京紫禁城的六倍之大，其建筑形制深刻影响了后世宫城建筑，奠定了中国2000余年宫城建筑的基本格局。

　　2014年6月22日，在卡塔尔多哈召开的联合国教科文组织第38届世界遗产大会上，汉长安城未央宫遗址作为中国、哈萨克斯坦和吉尔吉斯斯坦三国联合申遗的"丝绸之路：长安—天山廊道的路网"中的一处遗址点成功列入《世界遗产名录》。

夜如何其？夜未央，庭燎之光。
——《诗经·小雅·庭燎》

Weiyang Palace was the major imperial palace, the political center and national symbol of Western Han Dynasty. Built in the seventh year of Emperor Gaozu (200 B.C.) in Han Dynasty and supervised by Senior Minister Xiao He, it is located on Longshouyuan in the southwest corner of Chang'an City of Han Dynasty, also known as the Western Palace. Since the completion of Weiyang Palace, the emperors of Western Han Dynasty lived there and the palace became the center for issuing decrees in the Han Empire for more than 200 years. So Weiyang Palace became synonymous with Han Palace in the poems of later generations.

汉未央宫少府遗址 ⬠
Shaofu Site of Weiyang Palace in Han Dynasty

Weiyang Palace is the eastern starting point of the Silk Road, with a total area six times as large as the Forbidden City in Beijing. Its architectural form has profoundly influenced the later imperial city architecture and established the basic pattern of imperial city architecture in China for more than 2,000 years.

On June 22, 2014, at the 38th UNESCO World Heritage Committee meeting held in Doha, Qatar, the site of Weiyang Palace in Chang'an City of Han Dynasty was successfully listed in the World Heritage List as a site in the "Silk Road: Road Network of Chang'an-Tianshan Corridor" jointly applied by China, Kazakhstan and Kyrgyzstan.

九天阊阖开宫殿

Tang Dynasty: Great Prosperity and International Exchanges

公元 618 年李渊在长安称帝，建立唐朝。唐太宗继位后开创"贞观之治"，将中国传统农业社会推向鼎盛。唐玄宗即位后励精图治，开创了经济繁荣、四夷宾服、万邦来朝的"开元盛世"。唐朝成为古代中国的历史巅峰。

"九天阊阖开宫殿，万国衣冠拜冕旒"，高度强化的里坊空间格局、坊市治理制度，推动唐长安城跻身为中国乃至世界上第一个真正意义上的国际化大都市。同一时期，日本、渤海国循此规制，复刻了形制一致、体量微缩的京都城、奈良城和龙泉府，深化和加强了东亚儒家文化圈都城营建制度。

In 618 A.D., Li Yuan proclaimed himself emperor in Chang'an and established Tang Dynasty. After Emperor Taizong succeeded to the throne, he initiated the era of "Prosperity of Zhenguan", which pushed the Chinese traditional agricultural society to its peak. After Emperor Xuanzong acceded to the throne, he made great efforts and created the "Prosperity of Kaiyuan", which was characterized by economic prosperity, peace with neighboring countries and frequent exchanges with other nations. Tang Dynasty became the historical summit of ancient China.

"As soon as the royal palace opened its golden red gate, envoys from all over the world bowed to appear in court." The highly strengthened spatial pattern of residential areas and the strict governance system of alleys and markets promoted Chang'an City of Tang Dynasty to become the first truly international metropolis in China. In the same period, Japan and Bohai State followed this regulation, and built Kyoto City, Nara City and Longquanfu with the same shape and miniature size of Chang'an City, which deepened and strengthened the capital construction system of Confucian cultural circle in East Asia.

　　唐长安城完美体现了盛唐气象，作为当时世界上规模最大的城市和中国古代最大的都城，比同时期的东罗马帝国的都城君士坦丁堡大 7 倍。

　　唐长安城是在隋大兴城基础上建设而成。其由宫城、皇城与外郭城三部分组成，周长 36.7 千米，面积达 84 平方千米。宫城是皇帝居住和处理朝政之地，位于全城正中的北部，平面为长方形，东西长 2820 米，南北宽 1492 米，周长 8600 米。唐长安城一条南北中轴线纵贯全城，东西左右均衡对称，坊里排列如棋局。

Chang'an City in Tang Dynasty perfectly reflected the atmosphere of the prosperous Tang Dynasty. As the largest city in the world and the largest capital in ancient China at that time, it was 7 times larger than Constantinople, the capital of the Eastern Roman Empire at the same time.

Chang'an City in Tang Dynasty was built on the basis of Daxing City in Sui Dynasty. It consists of imperial city, royal city and outer city, with a circumference of 36.7 kilometers and an area of 84 square kilometers. Imperial city is the place where emperors lived and handled the state affairs. It is located in the north of the whole city, rectangular in shape, 2,820 meters long from east to west, 1,492 meters wide from north to south, and 8.6 kilometers in circumference. A north-south central axis of Chang'an City in Tang Dynasty runs through the whole city, which is balanced and symmetrical from east to west, and the residential quarters are arrayed like a chessboard.

百千家似围棋局，十二街如种菜畦。

——【唐】白居易《登观音台望城》（节选）

长安大道横九天，峨眉山月照秦川。

——【唐】李白

《峨眉山月歌送蜀僧晏入中京》（节选）

"大明"一词出自《诗经·大雅》中的《大明》，大明宫是大唐帝国的大朝正宫，唐朝的政治中心和国家象征，位于今西安北侧的龙首原，是唐长安城三座主要宫殿"三大内"（大明宫、太极宫、兴庆宫）中规模最大的一座，称为"东内"。自唐高宗起，先后有 17 位唐朝皇帝在此处理朝政，历时 200 余年 。

大明宫始建于唐太宗贞观八年（634），占地面积约 3.2 平方千米，整个宫域可分为前朝和内庭两部分。大明宫是当时全世界最辉煌壮丽的宫殿群，也是当时世界上面积最大的宫殿建筑群，号称"万宫之宫""东方圣殿"，被称为"中国宫殿建筑的巅峰之作"。正南门丹凤门被考古界誉为"盛唐第一门"，门前大街宽达 176 米，至今仍然是世界上最宽的街道。

2014 年 6 月 22 日，唐长安城大明宫遗址作为"丝绸之路：长安—天山廊道的路网"中的一处遗址点成功列入《世界遗产名录》。

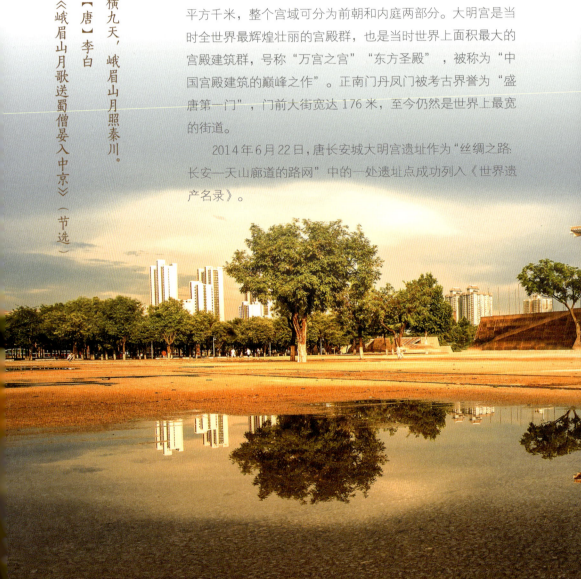

The word "Daming" comes from "Brightness" in The Book of Songs - Major Elegant Songs. Daming Palace, the political center and national symbol of Tang Dynasty, is located in Longshouyuan in the north of today's Xi'an. It is the largest of the three major palaces (Daming Palace, Taiji Palace and Xingqing Palace) in Chang'an City of Tang Dynasty, and is called "Dongnei" (east palace). Since Emperor Gaozong's time, there were 17 emperors of the Tang Dynasty handling the government affairs here, which lasted for more than 200 years.

Daming Palace was built in the eighth year of Zhenguan Period of Emperor Taizong (634), covering an area of about 3.2 square kilometers. The whole palace area can be divided into two parts: the front court and the inner court. Daming Palace was the most magnificent palace complex and also the largest palace complex in the world at that time, the so-called "palace of ten thousand palaces" and "oriental divine palace". It is now regarded as "the pinnacle of Chinese palace architecture". Danfeng Gate, the main southern gate, has been honored as "the first gate in the prosperous Tang Dynasty" by the cultural and archaeological community. The street in front of it is 176 meters wide and is still the widest street in the world.

On June 22nd, 2014, Daming Palace Site was successfully listed in the World Heritage List as a site in "Silk Road: Road Network of Chang'an-Tianshan Corridor".

大明宫国家遗址公园 ●
Daming Palace National Site Park

兴庆宫是唐长安城三大宫殿群之一，称为"南内"。位于长安外郭东城春明门内。兴庆宫内建有兴庆殿、南熏殿、大同殿、勤政务本楼、花萼相辉楼和沉香亭等建筑物。

兴庆宫公园建于 1958 年，是在原唐兴庆宫的遗址上兴建起来一座集文化娱乐与遗址保护于一体的西安市内最大的城市遗址公园。目前，唐兴庆宫公园综合提升项目主体改造已完成，2021 年 6 月底重新盛大开园迎客。

兴庆宫是唐玄宗做藩王时期的府邸，是唐玄宗开元、天宝时期的中国政治中心所在，也是他与爱妃杨玉环长期居住的地方。大诗人李白在兴庆宫留下千古名句："名花倾国两相欢，常得君王带笑看。"就是奉旨描述杨贵妃而作。

《酉阳杂俎》中记载："天宝初，安西道进娑罗枝……'特为奇绝，不庇凡草，不止恶禽，耸干无惭于松括，成荫不愧于桃李'……"相传，唐玄宗很喜爱娑罗树，便命人在兴庆宫内开辟一个娑罗园，种植这种有异香的娑罗树，"娑罗巷"由此演变而来。

云想衣裳花想容，春风拂槛露华浓。
若非群玉山头见，会向瑶台月下逢。
——【唐】李白《清平调（其一）》

Xingqing Palace is one of the three palace complexes in Chang'an City of Tang Dynasty, which is called "Nannei" (south place). Located inside Chunming Gate of eastern outer city of Chang'an, Xingqing Palace is built with Xingqing Hall, Nanxun Hall, Datong Hall, Diligence Tower, Calyx Tower and Fragrance Pavilion.

Xingqing Palace Park, built in 1958 on the original site, is the largest urban heritage park in Xi'an, which integrates culture, entertainment and heritage protection. At present, the transformation project of the comprehensive upgrading of Xingqing Palace Park of Tang Dynasty has been completed, and the park is to be re-opened at the end of June 2021.

Xingqing Palace, the residence of Emperor Xuanzong of Tang Dynasty when he was seignior, was the political center of China in Kaiyuan and Tianbao periods of Emperor Xuanzong, and the place where he and his concubine Yang Yuhuan lived for a long time. Li Bai, a great poet of Tang Dynasty, wrote in Xingqing Palace these eternal lines to describe Yang's good looks by following the emperor's decree: "The peerless beauty and the red peony set off each other's merits, which often makes the monarch keep smiling and watching."

Sketch-book of Stories records, "At the beginning of Tianbao Period, a sal tree (shorea robusta) was sent to the court from Anxi region... It was strange, never sheltering ordinary grass or deterring evil birds. It was as tall as a pine tree, and grew as quickly as peach and plum trees ..." According to legend, Emperor Xuanzong loved the sal tree so much that he ordered to open a special garden for planting sal trees with peculiar fragrance in Xingqing Palace.

绝胜宝藏满皇都

Eye-catching Treasures throughout the Ancient Capital

西安是"天然历史博物馆"，号称"文物甲天下"，不可移动文物景点有 2944 处，其中全国重点文物保护单位 41 处、省级文物保护单位 65 处、市级文物保护单位 184 处。种类繁多、体系完整的古迹遗址，数量巨大、地位特殊的馆藏文物，不仅是中国历史源远流长和生生不息的重要见证，也是保持和塑造西安城市特色，支撑和实现高质量发展的珍贵资源。

以陕西历史博物馆、西安博物院等大馆为带动，大唐西市博物馆、关中民俗艺术博物院等民间博物馆风起云涌，迄今西安共有博物馆 150 座，拥有国家一级博物馆 7 家，位列 15 个副省级前列。

Xi'an itself is a "natural history museum", boasting the fame of having "the best cultural relics in the world". There are 2,944 immovable cultural relic sites, including 41 national key cultural relic protection units, 65 provincial cultural relic protection units and 184 municipal cultural relic protection units. There are many kinds of historical sites with complete systems, and a large number of cultural relics with special status in the collection of cultural institutions, which are not only an important witness to the long and continuous history of China, but also valuable resources to maintain and shape the characteristics of Xi'an City, and to support and realize its high-quality development.

Driven by Shaanxi History Museum and Xi'an Museum, non-governmental museums such as Tang West Market Museum and Guanzhong Folk Art Museum are surging forward. Up to now, there are 150 museums in Xi'an, including 7 national first-class museums, which ranks among the top 15 sub-provincial level museums.

陕西历史博物馆正门
Front Gate of Shaanxi History Museum

陕西历史博物馆，中国第一座大型现代化国家级博物馆，国家一级博物馆，首批"AAAA"级旅游景点，被誉为"古都明珠，华夏宝库"。陕西历史博物馆被中国文物学会、中国建筑学会评选入"中国20世纪建筑遗产"，更被联合国教科文组织确认为世界一流博物馆。

陕西历史博物馆建筑的外观着意突出了盛唐风采，长安自古帝王都，历史上先后有周、秦、汉、隋、唐等13个封建王朝在此建都，具有丰富的地上地下文物，形成了陕西独特的历史文化风貌。其文物不仅数量多、种类全，而且品位高、价值广。收藏一级文物762件（组），国宝级文物18件（组），其中2件为首批禁止出国（境）展览文物，居中国博物馆前列。

Shaanxi History Museum, China's first large-scale modern national museum, national first-class museum, and one of the first batch of "AAAA" tourist attractions, is known as "the pearl of the ancient capital and the treasure house of China". Shaanxi History Museum is selected as "China's 20th Century Architectural Heritage" by China Cultural Relics Society and China Architectural Society, and recognized as a world-class museum by UNESCO.

The appearance of Shaanxi History Museum highlights the style of the prosperous Tang Dynasty. Chang'an has been the imperial capital since ancient times. Thirteen feudal dynasties, including Zhou Dynasty, Qin Dynasty, Han Dynasty, Sui Dynasty and Tang Dynasty, have established their capitals here in history. Xi'an is rich in above-ground and underground cultural relics, forming a unique historical and cultural style of Shaanxi. Its cultural relics are not only numerous and diverse, but also of high grade and wide value. There are 762 first-class cultural relics (groups) and 18 national treasure cultural relics (groups) in the collection, among which 2 are on the first batch of cultural relics prohibited from going abroad for exhibition, ranking the forefront of Chinese museums.

现藏陕西历史博物馆。

战国时秦国杜虎符，1973年因农民平整土地被发现，一度被当成小孩玩具。虎符是目前发现的中国最早的兵符。君主持半符，将领持半符，需要调兵的时候，使者携带君主之符前往将领的营寨，与将领之符契合得严丝合缝，则按命令立即出兵。现代汉语中的"符合"一词即来源于此。战国到秦汉时期，兵符多为虎形。

杜虎符印证了秦国在少陵原西周杜伯国（杜国）封地（今西安市东南）设杜县的历史，真实地反映了战国时期虎符调兵遣将制度的历史，这是我国现存最早的虎符实物。

Now it is in the collection of Shaanxi History Museum.

The bronze tiger-shaped tally of Qin State was discovered in 1975 on the site of Du during the Warring States Period by farmers who leveled the land, and it was once regarded as a toy for children. It is the earliest military symbol found in China. The monarch had one half while the general held the other half. When it was necessary to mobilize troops, the messenger carried the monarch's half of the tally to the general's camp. If this half could fit perfectly with the general's half, then he would dispatch his troops immediately according to the order. The word "conformity" in modern Chinese language is just derived from this operation. From Warring States to Qin and Han Dynasties, most of the military symbols were tiger-shaped.

The Bronze Tiger-shaped Tally of Du confirms the history of Qin State setting up Du County in Western Zhou Dynasty's Dubo State or Du State (now southeast of Xi'an) in Shaolingyuan, and truly reflects the history of the system of dispatching troops by using tiger-shaped tally during the Warring States Period. It is the earliest existing physical object of tally in China.

⌂ 秦·杜虎符
Qin Tiger-shaped Tally of Du

现藏陕西历史博物馆。汉高祖皇后吕雉的玉玺，1968年在咸阳的韩家湾公社韩家湾被 13 岁的小学生偶然捡到。西汉皇后之玺是汉代皇后玉玺的唯一实物资料，对研究秦汉帝后玺印有着十分重要的价值。

吕雉是中国历史上有记载的第一位皇后和皇太后。同时也是秦始皇统一中国，实行皇帝制度之后，第一个临朝称制的女性，被司马迁列入记录皇帝政事的本纪，后来班固作《汉书》仍然沿用。她开汉代外戚专权的先河。

Now it is in the collection of Shaanxi History Museum.The imperial jade deal of Emperor Gaozu's Queen Lü Zhi was picked up by a 13-year-old student in Hanjiawan in Xianyang in 1968. The seal is the only physical object of the imperial jade seal of the queen in Han Dynasty Queen, which is of great value to the study of the imperial seal of Qin and Han Dynasties.

Lü Zhi is the first recorded queen and empress dowager in the Chinese history. At the same time, after Emperor Qin Shihuang unified China and implemented the emperor system, she was the first woman who was given imperial titles and appeared in court. Historian Sima Qian listed her as one of the monarchs with biographic sketches to record the emperor's political affairs, and later Ban Gu still did the same in his Book of Han Dynasty. She sets a precedent in Han Dynasty for the exclusive power of consorts.

西汉·皇后之玺玉印

Imperial Jade Seal of the Queen in Western Han Dynasty

皇后玉玺，文与帝同。皇后之玺，金螭虎纽。

——《汉官旧仪》

西汉·皇后之玺玉印
Imperial Jade Seal of the Queen

现藏陕西历史博物馆。1970年出土于西安市何家村。利用玉料的俏色纹理雕琢而成。杯体为角状兽首形，兽双角为杯柄。嘴部镶金帽，眼、耳、鼻皆刻画细微精确。

这种酒具常出现在游牧民族的宴饮场面中，唐朝贵族以追求新奇为时尚，李白所谓"落花踏尽游何处，笑入胡姬酒肆中"。也许就用的这种类型的酒杯。《旧唐书》中有"开元十六年大康国献兽首玛瑙杯"的记载。唐兽首玛瑙杯是至今所见的唐代唯一一件俏色玉雕，是唐代玉器做工最精湛的一件，也是唐代中外文化交流的产物。

The agate cup is now in the collection of Shaanxi History Museum. It was unearthed in Hejia Village, Xi'an, in 1970. It's carved out of jade with pretty-colored texture. The cup body is of angular animal head, with animal horns as the cup handles. The mouth is inlaid with a gold cover, and the eyes, ears and nose are all carved with fine precision.

This kind of wine vessels often appears in the banquet scene of people from the western regions. The aristocrats in Tang Dynasty pursued novelty as the fashion. Li Bai once wrote, "Where do they like to go after enjoying flowers in spring? They often drink and laugh in an alien's pub for fun." Maybe they just used this type of wine vessels to drink wine. In Book of Old Tang Dynasty, there is a record of "the animal-headed agate cup presented by Dakang State as a tribute in the 16th year of Kaiyuan". The animal-headed agate cup is the only beautiful jade carving from Tang Dynasty ever seen so far. It is the most exquisite jade work in Tang Dynasty and the product of cultural exchanges between China and foreign countries at that time.

⚬ 陕西历史博物馆镇馆之宝——镶金兽首玛瑙杯
Treasure of Shaanxi History Museum – Animal-headed Agate Cup Inlaid with Gold

西安博物院是国家一级博物馆，馆内有唐代千年古塔小雁塔及长安八景之一的"雁塔晨钟"。该博物院是集博物馆、名胜古迹、城市公园为一体的独特历史文化场馆。西安博物院整体外观以天圆地方理念创作，突出体现中国传统文化思想。博物院收藏了西安各个历史时期的文物 13 万件，其中拥有国家三级以上珍贵文物 14400 多件，鎏金铜铺首、龙纹空心砖、陶水管道、釉陶望楼、三彩院落模型等都是其中的精品。

Xi'an Museum is a national first-class museum, with the ancient Xiao yan Pagoda of Tang Dynasty and the "Morning Bell of Xiao yan Pagoda", one of the eight attractions in Chang'an. The museum is a unique historical and cultural venue integrating museums, historical sites and urban parks. The overall structure of Xi'an Museum is created with the concept of orbicular sky and rectangular earth, which highlights the traditional Chinese culture. The Museum has a collection of 130,000 cultural relics from various historical periods in Xi'an, among which there are more than 14,400 precious cultural relics of national grade 3 or above, among which gold-plated bronze doorknob, dragon-pattern hollow bricks, pottery water pipes, glazed pottery watchtower and tri-colored courtyard model are all finest works.

西安博物院全景
Panorama of Xi'an Museum

仍羽人于丹丘兮，留不死之旧乡。

——【战国】屈原《楚辞·远游》（节选）

现藏西安博物院。1964 年西安市未央区南玉丰村汉城遗址出土。青铜羽人像最为特别之处在于背部斜伸出的羽翼，以及大腿和膝盖饰有排列紧凑的鳞状垂羽。从人像背生双翼及所施羽状纹饰来看，它展现的正是中国古代传说中的羽人形象。"羽人"是我国艺术发展史上出现的一种造型奇特且广泛流传的人鸟合体形象，它是古代人们希望超越自然现实，追求自身本能突破的想象产物，寄托着先民对神话理想、宗教世界的一种精神向往。中国的神仙传说起源很早，秦汉时期尤盛，其中就有讲述人们修行成仙后，长出羽翼飞到天上的传说。

The bronze winged man is now in the collection of Xi'an Museum. In 1964, it was unearthed at Hancheng Site in Nanyufeng Village, Weiyang District, Xi'an. The most special feature of the bronze figure is that the wings extend obliquely from the back, and the thighs and knees are decorated with tightly arranged scaly feathers. From the pattern of wings on its back and feather-like ornamentation, it shows the image of winged man in ancient Chinese legends. "Winged Man" is a peculiar and widely spread image of man and bird combined in the history of art development in China. It is an imaginary product of ancient people's desire to transcend natural reality and pursue their own instinctive breakthrough, and it sustains the ancestors' spiritual yearning for mythological ideals and religious world. Chinese fairy tales originated very early, and thrived especially in Qin and Han Dynasties. Among them, there are legends about people who have wings and fly to the sky after becoming immortals.

青铜羽人
Bronze Winged Man

唐代密檐式砖塔——小雁塔
Dense-eaved Brick Tower — Small Wild Goose Pagoda of Tang Dynasty

现藏西安博物院。1966 年西安市莲湖区制药厂唐墓出土。作者通过骏马奔跃的瞬间捕捉，体现骏马神勇彪悍的内在精神。这件胡人腾空马造型精美，釉色鲜亮细腻，成为唐三彩中少见的精品。

汉武帝元鼎四年（前 113）秋，有个名叫"暴利长"的敦煌囚徒，在当地捕得一匹汗血宝马献给汉武帝。汉武帝得到此马后，欣喜若狂，称其为"天马"。并作歌曰："太一贡兮天马下，沾赤汗兮沫流赭。骋容与兮跇万里，今安匹兮龙为友。"

女为胡妇学胡妆，伎进胡音务胡乐。

——【唐】元稹

《和李校书新题乐府十二首·法曲》（节选）

The tri-colored pottery nomad on a galloping horse of Tang Dynasty is now in the collection of Xi'an Museum. It was unearthed from a Tang Dynasty tomb in Lianhu Pharmaceutical Factory in Xi'an in 1966. Through the instant capture of the galloping horse, its maker vividly reflects the inner spirit of the horse - bold and tough. This nomad's galloping horse is exquisite in shape and bright and delicate in glaze color, making it a rare boutique among the tri-colored pottery figures of Tang Dynasty.

In the autumn of the fourth year of Emperor Yuanding of Han Dynasty (113 B.C.), a Dunhuang prisoner named "Baolizhang" caught a ferghana horse in the local area and presented it to Emperor Wudi of Han Dynasty. After Emperor Wudi got this horse, he was ecstatic and called it "Tianma" (heavenly horse). He also wrote a song saying, "The Lord of Heaven rewards us with a horse sent to our world. Its body is soaked with sweat flowing like red bubbles; when galloping it may travel a thousand li in a short while. Once a friend of the dragon's in holy heaven, it now feels at ease to be a horse on earth."

西安博物院镇馆之宝——三彩胡人腾空马
Treasure in Xi'an Museum – Tri-colored Galloping Horse

长安古道马迟迟

Magnificent Buildings of the Ancient Times

从十三朝到西北重镇，宋元明清，明城墙、钟鼓楼、北院门，这些不可移动的建筑文物，依然为这座千年古都雕刻时光之美。

西安城墙
Xi'an City Wall

As the capital of 13 dynasties and then a city of strategic importance in the northwest regions, Xi'an boasts the possession of many immovable architectural relics such as the Ming City Wall, the Bell and Drum Towers, and the North Courtyard Gate from Song, Yuan, Ming and Qing Dynasties. These buildings are still preserving the beauty of time for this millennium ancient capital.

西安城墙是我国现存最完整、规模最大的古代城垣建筑。

唐朝以后，西安虽然不再是中国的都城，但仍是具有军事战略意义的西北重镇和西北地区的政治经济文化中心。宋代西安属永兴路京兆府，元代属奉元路。明洪武二年（1369），改奉元路为西安府，取意"安定西北"，西安之名由此而来。明朝时在隋唐长安城的基础上建成了规模宏大坚固的城墙，周长13.79千米，平面为长方形，形成了今天西安城的格局。

西安城墙是西安的固有骨架，它对西安的意义，正像梁思成先生说的那样，不只是一堆平凡叠积的砖堆，更是这个城市的文化象征。

从民国时期开始，为方便人们出入古城区，西安城先后新辟了多座城门，如今西安城墙已有城门18座。1961年，西安城墙被公布为全国重点文物保护单位，近年来，南门迎宾，成为接待外国政要、贵宾的重要外交礼仪。

西北望长安，可怜无数山。

——【宋】辛弃疾《菩萨蛮·书江西造口壁》（节选）

Xi'an City Wall is the most complete and largest existing ancient city wall in China.

After Tang Dynasty, although Xi'an was no longer the capital of China, it was still an important city with strategic military significance and the political, economic and cultural center of Northwest China. Xi'an belonged to Capital Distrct of Yongxing Region in Song Dynasty and to Fengyuan Region in Yuan Dynasty. In the second year of Hongwu Period in Ming Dynasty (1369), Fengyuan Region was changed to Xi'an Prefecture, meaning "stablizing the northwest", hence the name of Xi'an. During Ming Dynasty, a large-scale and solid city wall was built on the basis of Chang'an City in Sui and Tang Dynasties, with a circumference of 13.79 kilometers and a rectangular plane, forming the pattern of today's Xi'an City.

Xi'an City Wall is the inherent skeleton of Xi 'an, and of great significance to Xi'an. Just as Mr. Liang Sicheng said, Xi' an City Wall is not only a pile of ordinary stacked bricks, but a cultural symbol of the city.

Since the Republic of China, in order to facilitate people's access to the ancient city, many new gates have successively been opened, and now there are 18 gates in the city wall. In 1961, Xi'an City Wall was declared as a national key cultural relic protection unit. In recent years, the ceremony of welcoming guests at the South Gate has become an important diplomatic etiquette for receiving foreign dignitaries and distinguished guests.

钟楼
Bell Tower

西安钟楼是西安城的地标建筑，位于明城墙内东西南北四条大街的交汇处，是中国现存钟楼中形制最大、保存最完整的一座。昔日楼上悬一口大钟，用于报警报时，故名"钟楼"。

钟楼建于明太祖洪武十七年（1384），初建于今广济街口，与鼓楼相对，明神宗万历十年（1582）整体迁移于今址。

钟楼建在方型基座之上，为砖木结构，重楼三层檐，四角攒顶的形式，总高 36 米，占地面积 1377 平方米。西安历史上第一家电影院就开设于钟楼。

钟楼曾悬挂的是铸造于唐代的被誉为"天下第一名钟"的景云钟。景云钟铸成于唐景云二年（711），唐睿宗李旦亲自为其撰书铭文，钟高 2 米，直径达 1.5 米，重达万斤，钟身鹤飞龙翔，钟鸣声扬数十里，一直为西大街广济街口的皇家道观景龙观（后改称迎祥观）所用。中央人民广播电台曾对景云钟进行录音，中央电视台春节联欢晚会每年除夕之夜作为辞旧迎新的"新年钟声"进行播放。现悬挂于钟楼西北角的是复制品。

居人耳传，谓明建是楼，以徙景龙观钟。

——【清】张楷《重修西安钟楼记》（节选）

Xi'an Bell Tower, a landmark of Xi'an, is located at the intersection of four streets - east, west, north and south - within the Ming City Wall. It is the largest and best-preserved bell tower in China. In the past, there was a giant bell hanging upstairs, which was used to alarm and tell the time, hence the name "Bell Tower".

Bell Tower was built in the 17th year of Hongwu Period of Emperor Taizu of Ming Dynasty (1384), originally at Guangji Street, just opposite to Drum Tower, and then moved to today's site in the 10th year of Wanli Period of Emperor Shenzong of Ming Dynasty (1582).

The bell tower, built on a square base, is of brick-wood structure, with three layers of eaves and four corners, and with a total height of 36 meters and an area of 1,377 square meters. The first cinema in Xi'an history was opened in the bell tower.

Jingyun Bell, which was cast in Tang Dynasty and is known as "the first bell in the world", was once hung in the bell tower. Jingyun Bell was cast in the second year of Jingyun Period of Tang (711), and Emperor Ruizong, Li Dan, personally wrote an inscription for it. Thebell is 2 meters high, 1.5 meters in diameter and weighs 10,000 kilograms. The bell is carved with flying crane and soaring dragon. When the bell rings, its sound could be heard many miles away. It belonged to royal Jinglong Temple (later renamed Yingxiang Temple) at Guangji Street in West Street. China National Radio once recorded the sound of Jingyun Bell, and CCTV Spring Festival Gala replays it as the "New Year's Bell Ringing" every year to bid farewell to the old and welcome the new. Now hanging in the northwest corner of the bell tower is a replica.

● 钟楼
Bell Tower

鼓楼

Drum Tower

西府层楼接上台，客怀落日为谁开。
一天秋色云飞断，万户晴辉鹊噪来。

——【明】殷奎《登西安府鼓楼》（节选）

西安鼓楼始建于明洪武十三年（1380），比钟楼早建4年 。楼上原有巨鼓一面，每日击鼓报时，故称"鼓楼"。鼓楼横跨北院门大街之上，和钟楼相距仅200米，互相对应。 主持修建鼓楼的人是长兴侯耿炳文、西安知府王宗周，据说是在微雨朦胧之中为鼓楼工程奠基的。

在鼓楼第三檐下，南北各悬匾额一块，南面为"文武盛地"，北匾为"声闻于天"。楼内设有楼梯，登临楼上，凭栏便能眺望全城景色。

西安鼓楼是中国现存明代建筑中仅次于故宫太和殿、长陵棱恩殿的一座大体量的古代建筑，且在中国同类建筑中年代最久、保存最完好，属于同类建筑之冠。

Xi'an Drum Tower was built in the 13th year of Hongwu Period in Ming Dynasty (1380), 4 years before Bell Tower. Upstairs, there is a huge drum, which is beaten every day to tell the time, so it is called Drum Tower. Drum Tower spans over Beiyuanmen Street, only 200 meters away from Bell Tower, corresponding to each other. The people who presided over the construction of Drum Tower were Marquis Geng Bingwen of Changxing and Magistrate Wang Zongzhou of Xi'an, who allegedly laid the foundation stone for Drum Tower project in the light rain.

Under the third eaves of Drum Tower, two plaques hang on both sides, respectively with the inscriptions of "Land of Civil and Military Prosperity" on the south and "Voice Heard by Heaven" on the north. There are stairs in the tower, and one can have an overview of the whole city by climbing to the top floor.

Xi'an Drum Tower is a massive ancient building which is next only to the Hall of Supreme Harmony in the Forbidden City and Leng'en Hall in Changling Mauseleum among the existing Ming Dynasty buildings in China. It is the oldest and best-preserved building of its kind in China, and ranks first among similar buildings.

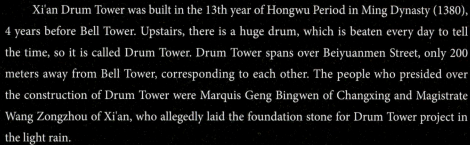

鼓楼 ●
Drum Tower

长安阡陌自咸宁

Intertwining Alleys Reminiscent of the Past

　　街巷，是一座城市的脉络。老街巷，就如同一座城市的根，饱含着城市居民的情感记忆，体现着城市的文化品位。古都西安的街巷，如炭市街、甜水井、湘子庙街、大车家巷、桥梓口、红庙坡、庙后街、大差市等，处处有故事。

　　截至 2021 年 5 月底，西安市完成了包括莲湖区北院门历史文化街区 37 条街巷在内的 599 条背街小巷提升改造任务。改造工作以治理脏、乱、差等问题为切入点，注重功能完善，并且充分挖掘街巷文化底蕴、留存城市记忆、传承历史文脉、提升文化品位。

● 骡马市步行街
Luomashi the street of way

Streets and alleys are the venation of a city. Old streets and alleys, just like the roots of a city, contain the emotional memories of urban residents and embody the cultural taste of the city. There are stories everywhere in the streets and alleys of Xi'an, the ancient capital, such as Tanshi Street, Tianshuijing Street, Xiangzimiao Street, Dajiajia Lane, Qiaozikou, Hongmiaopo, Miaohou Street, Dachashi, etc.

By the end of May, 2021, Xi'an had completed the upgrading and reconstruction of 599 back streets and alleys, including 37 streets and alleys in Beiyuanmen historical and cultural block of Lianhu District. All the transformation work takes the problems of dirty, chaotic and poor conditions as the breakthrough point, pays attention to the perfection of functions, fully explores the cultural heritage of the streets and alleys, preserves the memories of the city, inherits its historical legacies and promotes the cultural taste of the whole city.

骡马市

Luomashi

　　骡马市是西安著名的商业中心，位于西安市东大街东段南侧，北起东大街，南至东木头市。骡马市长612米，宽7米。全街由5条巷子组成，这5条巷子从北向南依次是水车巷、肋子巷（中华人民共和国成立后改为西柳巷）、马王庙巷、戴家巷、惠家巷。此街原为唐长安城少府监所在地，唐末以后渐为居民坊巷。唐代这个地区叫"耳窝坊"，骡马市街市的形成应是在明万历末期。明《西安府城图》有记载，明代嘉靖二十一年（1542），这里是牲畜交易市场，据此推算，骡马市这条古老街道的名称，到现在已有400余年的历史了。东北侧原南柳巷小学是唐朝开国元勋尉迟敬德的府第。清末慈禧太后西狩西安，曾在这里放过舍饭。

Luomashi is a famous commercial center in Xi'an. It is located on the southern side of the east section of Xi'an East Street, starting from East Street in the north to Dongmutoushi in the south. Luomashi is 612 meters long and seven meters wide. The whole street consists of five alleys, which are "Shuiche Alley, Leizi Alley (changed to Xiliux Alley after liberation), Mawangmiao Alley, Daijia Alley and Huijia Alley" from north to south. This street was originally the government office of Shaofu Supervisor in Chang'an City of Tang Dynasty, and gradually became a residential alley after the end of Tang Dynasty. In Tang Dynasty, this area was called "Erwo Quarter", and the market of Luomashi was formed at the end of Wanli Period in Ming Dynasty. It is recorded in the City Map of Xi'an Prefecture in Ming Dynasty that livestock trading markets were everywhere in the 21st year of Jiajing Period in Ming Dynasty (1542), which is the earliest document found. Based on this, it is estimated that the name of this ancient street of Luomashi has a history of more than 400 years. The former Nanliuxiang Primary School in the northeast used to be the official residence of General Yuchi Jingde, one of the founders of Tang Dynasty. In the late Qing Dynasty, Empress Dowager Cixi fled to Xi'an, and gave alms to the public here in this place.

下马陵 Xiamaling

说起下马陵，必然会提及一个人，那就是汉代著名的改革家董仲舒。下马陵其名缘起于此处的董仲舒墓，其间董仲舒墓文保碑上记载："昔汉武帝每幸芙蓉苑，至董仲舒墓下马。"于是民间称这里为下马陵。但是陕西话中"下马"二字与"虾蟆"同音，几经流传，便唤作"虾蟆陵"。

Xiama Ling is closely related to Dong Zhongshu, a famous reformer in Han Dynasty. The name of Xiama Mausoleum originated from Dong Zhongshu's tomb here. These words are inscribed on the protection stele of Dong Zhongshu's tomb: "In the past, every time when Emperor Wudi of Han Dynasty visited Furong (Lotus) Garden, he would dismount his horse in front of Dong Zhongshu's tomb." Therefore, people call it Xiama Mausoleum, literally "horse-dismounting mausoleum". However, the word "xiama" (dismounting a horse) in Shaanxi dialect has the same sound as "hama" (frog), so it is called "frog mausoleum" by the locals.

唐代宗广德年间（763—764），郭子仪从甘肃泾川返归长安之时，有西域各部将官等200余人随从班师回京，被安置于唐皇城内礼部衙署所处坊内，同时还为他们重修了长安"西大寺"（大学习巷清真寺）。他们在长安生活期间，学习唐朝的一切法令、制度和汉儒文化礼仪，而且也为中华文化和伊斯兰文化的交流奠定了基础，所以该坊被称为"学习巷"沿袭至今。米芾、董其昌在此留下墨宝，郑和也曾到访此地，这条千年古街生动呈现了中华民族对文化多样性、文明多元化的包容态度。

During the Guangde Period of Emperor Daizong of Tang Dynasty (763-764), when General Guo Ziyi returned to Chang'an from Jingchuan, Gansu Province, in the company of more than 200 people, including generals and officials from various western states, they were placed in the quarter where the offices of the Ministry of Rites were located inside the Royal City. At the same time, Chang'an "West Grand Mosque" (Daxuexi Alley Mosque) was rebuilt for them. During their stay in Chang'an, they learned all the laws and regulations of Tang Dynasty and the cultural etiquette of the Han people and Confucianism, which laid the foundation for the exchange of Chinese culture with Islamic culture. So this quarter was called "Xuexixi Alley" (meanig "learning alley"). The name has continued to be used ever since. Mi Fu and Dong Qichang left great paintings here, and the famous Chinese Navigator Zheng He also visited this place. This millennium ancient street vividly displays the Chinese nation's tolerant attitude towards cultural diversity and civilization pluralism.

大学习巷
Daxuexi Alley

粉巷

Fenxiang Alley

　　粉巷仅有 329 米长，而它的名字却为西安人所熟知。其得名一说以前粉巷是西安城的粮食一条街。据说街道上撒满厚厚的粉面，由此得名。第二种说法是粉巷是以卖胭脂得名，离得很远就能闻到浓浓的胭脂味道。还有一种是说粉巷是当初皇上选妃子的街道，因为西安是当年的国都，每年粉巷住满了进城等待被选的妃子，她们的身上有好闻的脂粉味。如今，粉巷利用其得天独厚的地理位置发展成为城市著名时尚街区，娱乐圣地。其中以酒吧街德福巷最出名。

　　Fenxiang Alley is only 329 meters long, but its name is well known to Xi 'an people. Fenxiang Alley was so named for three reasons: first, it used to be a place selling grains in Xi'an, so the street was all covered with a thick layer of flour; second, it was once a place selling rouge, something like a cosmetics street today, and one could smell strongly the rouge when passing by; third, Fenxiang was the street where the emperor selected concubines. Since Xi'an was the capital at that time, so every year Fenxiang was crowded with would-be concubines waiting to be chosen for the emperors, and their bodies gave off a good smell of rouge powder. Fenxiang has taken advantage of its unique geographical location to develop into a famous fashion block and entertainment center in the city. It is famous of the bar street Defu Alley.

元代时这里因药店密集，故十字口与今天的南广济街统称为药市街。虽然五味什字叫"什字"，它并非纵横交错的十字路口，实际上只是个东西向的街道。

其得名为"五味什字"相传是有段小故事的。

话说明清两代直至民国初年，这条街道曾开设过众多药铺，生意非常兴隆。比较著名的药店有藻露堂（创办于明朝天启二年，即公元1622年。该店以妇科良药"培坤丸"享誉省内外）、复元成、树仁堂、万年堂等。因我国医药自古讲究"四气五味"，其中"五味"指"甘、辛、酸、苦、咸"，街道因此而得"五味"之名。

Because of the dense gathering of pharmacies in Yuan Dynasty, Shizikou and Nanguangji Street today are collectively called drug market street. Although Wuwei (five-flavor) Crossroads is so called, it is not at all a criss-crossing intersection, but in fact, it is just an east-west street.

Its name "Wuwei Crossroads" is said to have a story.

It is said that from the Ming and Qing dynasties to the early years of the Republic of China, many drug stores were opened in this street, and the business was very prosperous. The most famous pharmacies were Zaolutang (founded in the second year of the Tianqi Period of Ming Dynasty, that is, A.D. 1622 and famous for its gynecological medicine "Peikun Pill"), Fuyuancheng, Shurentang and Wanniantang. Because the traditional Chinese medicine has paid special attention to "four qi and five flavors" since ancient times, among which "five flavors" refer to "sweet, pungent, sour, bitter and salty", the street has been named "five flavors".

红旗漫卷西风劲
Glorious Revolutionary Flag Still Being Carried Forward

血肉铸就长城，浇灌信念。葛牌镇区苏维埃政府纪念馆、八路军西安办事处、西安事变纪念馆、中共中央西北局等一批红色遗址见证志士仁人在西安城为理想社会奋斗的矫健身影，给予这座城青春无悔的深刻印记。

● 革命公园
  Revolution Park

Flesh and blood can cast the great wall and nourish the faith. A number of red revolutionary sites and relics, such as the District Soviet Government Memorial Museum at Gepai Town, the Eighth Route Army Xi'an Office, the Xi'an Incident Memorial Museum and the Northwest Bureau of the Communist Party of China Central Committee, have all witnessed the vigorous figures of the people with lofty faiths struggling for an ideal society in Xi 'an City, giving the city a deep imprint of youth with no regrets.

1934 年农历腊月二十九日，红二十五军连夜急行军，于大年三十黎明时，出其不意赶到葛牌街，直扑郑效仁民团一支队队部，除少数人逃出外，大部分当场做了俘房。接着红军按事先已侦察好的名单，分头逮捕了联保主任鲍学义、逢源号掌柜郭继荣等土豪劣绅共十多人。

初驻葛牌镇时，红军战士只能在空场院或房檐下搭草铺休息，尽管大多身穿单衣，脚穿草鞋，在数九隆冬的冰地里冻得直打哆嗦，但没有一个人进屋取暖，仅围着一堆柴火，直到天明。红军的宣传队分头向群众演说，还用麻头做的大笔，在墙上写满了标语。住在各家的战士主动给群众拾柴、扫院落、担水、磨面，女卫生员给群众看病送药。

1935 年 2 月，长征入陕的中国工农红军第二十五军在徐海东、程子华、吴焕先等领导下，创建了关中地区第一个红色政权——蓝田县葛牌镇区苏维埃政府，为配合中央红军战略转移做出了卓越贡献。葛牌镇区苏维埃政府纪念馆地处秦岭深处的蓝田县葛牌镇，这里也是关中地区最早的红色革命根据地。

附近有红二十五军文公岭战斗遗址纪念碑、红二十五军野战医院旧址、蓝洛革命根据地旧址、蓝田游击队活动遗址、汪锋同志故居纪念馆、红七十四师秦岭北麓活动遗址等红色遗迹，镌刻着红军当年枪林弹雨的艰苦岁月。

On the 29th day of the twelfth lunar month in 1934, the Red 25th Army marched swiftly overnight. At the dawn of the New Year's Eve, it rushed to Gepai Street by surprise, and went straight for a team of Zheng Xiaoren's militia. Except a few people who had escaped, all of them were captured on the spot. Then the Red Army separately arrested Bao Xueyi, the director of joint security, Guo Jirong, the boss of Fengyuan Store, and other local tyrants and evil gentry, totaling more than 10 people, according to the pre-reconnaissance list.

When they first settled in Gepai Town, the Red Army soldiers could only rest in the open yard or under the eaves for the night. Although most of them wore thin clothes and sandals and shivered with cold in the middle of winter, no one went into the peasants' houses to keep warm, only to sit by a pile of bonfire until dawn. The publicity team of the Red Army separately addressed the masses, and with crude brushes made of hemp heads, painted slogans on the walls. Soldiers residing in various families took the initiative to collect firewood, sweep courtyards, fetch water and grind grains for the local people, while the female health workers gave medical treatment and medicines to them.

In February 1935, under the leadership of Xu Haidong, Cheng Zihua and Wu Huanxian, the 25th Army of the Chinese Workers' and Peasants' Red Army, entered Shaanxi in the Long March and established the first red political power in Guanzhong area, the District Soviet Government in Gepai Town, Lantian County, which made outstanding contributions to the strategic advancement of the Central Red Army. The District Soviet Government Memorial Musem is located in Gepai Town, Lantian County, deep in the Qinling Mountains, which is the site of the earliest red revolutionary base in Guanzhong area.

Adjacent to the Memorial Museum, there are red relics such as the Red 25th Army Wengongling Battle Site Monument, the Red 25th Army Field Hospital Site, the Lanluo Revolutionary Base Site, the Lantian Guerrilla Activity Site, the Memorial Hall of Comrade Wang Feng's Former Residence, and the Red 74th Division's Qinling North Foothill Activity Site, all recording the hard years of the Red Army.

关中最早的革命根据地 —— 葛牌镇
Gepai Town - the Earliest Revolutionary Base in Guanzhong

　　1935 年前后，在民族危机空前严重的关头，蒋介石仍旧坚持"攘外必先安内"政策，张学良与中国共产党周恩来同志在延安举行会谈。与此同时，杨虎城收到了毛泽东同志派人给他送来的亲笔信。1936 年 12 月初，蒋介石亲临西安，下榻于临潼华清池，张学良多次对蒋"苦谏"，均痛遭拒绝。蒋介石限他三天内答复是否继续执行"剿共"的命令，否则将他和杨虎城的东、西北军调离陕西。张学良、杨虎城被迫于1936 年 12 月 12 日对蒋介石实行了"兵谏"，爆发了震惊中外的"西安事变"。

　　在中共中央和周恩来等人的努力下，最终达成了"停止内战，一致对外"的两党共识，开始了国共第二次合作，成为艰苦卓绝的抗日战争中关键的历史转折点。西安事变旧址是全国重点文物保护单位，由张学良公馆、西安事变指挥部、新城黄楼、杨虎城止园别墅、高桂滋公馆、西京招待所、华清池五间厅、兵谏亭等 8 处文物保护单位组成。

　　Around 1935, when the national crisis was unprecedentedly severe, Chiang Kai-shek still insisted on the policy of "stablizing the country before resisting the aggression". Later, Zhang Xueliang held talks with Comrade Zhou Enlai of the Communist Party of China in Yan'an. At the same time, Yang Hucheng received a personal letter from Comrade Mao Zedong. At the beginning of December, 1936, Chiang Kai-shek visited Xi'an in person and stayed at Huaqing Pool in Lintong. Zhang Xueliang repeatedly "remonstrated" verbally with Chiang Kai-shek and was bitterly rejected. Chiang Kai-shek gave him three days to reply as to whether to continue to carry out the order of "exterminating the Communist forces"; otherwise, Zhang Xueliang's and Yang Hucheng's northeast and northwest armies would be transferred from

Shaanxi. Zhang Xueliang and Yang Hucheng were forced to "remonstrate with Chiang Kai-shek by force" on December 12, 1936, and "Xi 'an Incident" broke out.

It was in the end settled peacefully and ended with a consensus of "stopping the civil war and unanimously resisting the Japanese aggression", which marked the beginning of the second cooperation between the Kuomintang and the Communist Party. Xi'an Incident became a key historical turning point in the arduous War of Resistance against Japanese Aggression. The former revolutionary site of Xi'an Incident is a national key cultural relic protection unit, which consists of 8 cultural relic protection subunits, including Zhang Xueliang Mansion, Xijing Guest House, Xi'an Incident Command, Xincheng Yellow Building, Yang Hucheng's Zhiyuan Villa, Gao Guizi Mansion, Xijing Guest House, Five-room Hall of Huaqing Pool and Armed Remonstrance Pavilion.

八路军西安办事处位于西安市新城区北新街七贤庄内。七贤庄始建于 1934 年冬，1936 年春建成并对外出租。七贤庄共有 10 座坐北朝南、自西向东排列的四合院式建筑，是国共第二次合作时期，中国共产党和八路军在国民党管辖区西安设立的公开办事机构。在全国数十个八路军办事处中成立最早，撤离最晚，影响最大。1988 年被列为全国重点文物保护单位。2015 年 8 月，被国务院批准公布列入第二批 100 处国家级抗战纪念设施遗址名录。

西安事变和平解决后，1937 年 2 月，经国共两党谈判同意，在西安设立半公开的红军联络处，七贤庄 1 号的大门外墙挂起了"国民革命军第十七路第三十八教导队通讯训练班"的牌子。

抗日战争时期，驻西安办事处利用其特殊的政治地位和地理位置，在维护和推动全民族抗日运动的发展，宣传中国共产党的抗日主张、开展统一战线工作，为八路军领取、采买、转运物资，输送爱国青年奔赴延安等方面做了大量卓有成效的工作，被誉为"红色堡垒""红色兵站"和"红色桥梁"。

The Eighth Route Army Office in Shaanxi is located in Qixianzhuang, Beixin Street, Xincheng District, Xi'an City. Qixianzhuang was built in the winter of 1934, completed in the spring of 1936 and rented out. Qixianzhuang has 10 quadrangle-style buildings facing south from west to east. It is an open office set up in Xi'an by the Communist Party of China and the Eighth Route Army under the Kuomintang's jurisdiction during the second cooperation period between the Kuomintang and the Communist Party of China. Among dozens of offices of the Eighth Route Army in China, the Xi'an office was established at the earliest, evacuated at the latest and had the greatest influence. In 1988, it was listed as a national key cultural relic protection unit. In August, 2015, it was approved by the State Council to be listed on the second batch of 100 state-level memorial facilities for the War of Resistance against Japanese Aggression.

After the peaceful settlement of Xi'an Incident, in February 1937, with the agreement of the Kuomintang and the Communist Party, a semi-public liaison office of the Red Army was set up in Xi'an, and the sign "Communication Training Class of the 38th Training Team of the 17th Route National Revolutionary Army" was hung on the outer wall of the gate of No.1 Qixianzhuang.

During the War of Resistance against Japanese Aggression, the office in Xi'an took advantage of its special political status and geographical position to maintain and promote the development of the whole nation's anti-Japanese movement by publicizing the anti-Japanese proposition of the Communist Party of China, carrying out the united front work, collecting and purchasing and transporting materials for the Eighth Route Army, and transporting patriotic youth to Yan'an, hence such titles as "Red Fortress", "Red Station" and "Red Bridge".

八路军西安办事处纪念馆 ▼
Eighth Route Army Xi'an Office

西安情报处（简称"西情处"），是中共中央社会部直接领导的情报机构，是党在西北乃至北方地区重要的情报机构。创建于 1939 年，正式定名于 1945 年，结束于 1949 年，前后共计 10 年，主要负责人是王超北，10 年间，西情处发展成 100 多人的庞大情报组织。在西安市内先后架设 8 部秘密电台，建立了两个传递情报的秘密交通站，开辟了通往延安和重庆的 3 个秘密交通线，护送大批干部和爱国人士，传送大量秘密资料。为保卫党组织、营救被捕同志、掩护并支援八路军西安办事处、保卫延安、解放西北和保护文化古都西安等方面做出重要贡献。

1949 年后，彭德怀曾带领苏联军事代表团参观这个秘密工作站。彭德怀评价："这个地下秘密室，曲里拐弯，设计巧妙，这是中国共产党革命事业进行艰苦奋斗的一个历史见证。"

Xi'an Intelligence Office (referred to as "Western Intelligence Office") is an intelligence agency directly led by the Department of Social Affairs of the CPC Central Committee and an important intelligence agency of the Party in the northwest and even in the north. This office was founded in 1939, officially named in 1945, and ended in 1949. The main person chiefly in charge was Wang Chaobei. In the 10 years, the Western Intelligence Office developed into a huge intelligence organization with more than 100 people. Eight secret radio stations were set up in Xi 'an, two secret traffic stations were set up to transmit intelligence, and three secret traffic lines were opened to Yan'an and Chongqing, escorting a large number of cadres and patriots and transmitting a large amount of secret information. It made important contributions to defending the party organizations, rescuing arrested comrades, covering and supporting the Eighth Route Army Office in Xi 'an, defending Yan'an, liberating the northwest and protecting the ancient cultural capital of Xi'an.

After 1949, General Peng Dehuai accompanied the Soviet Union military delegation to visit this former secret workstation. Peng commented: "This underground secret room, with its twists and turns and ingenious design, is a historical witness to the arduous struggle of the revolutionary cause of the Communist Party of China."

中共西安情报处奇园茶社旧址纪念碑 ⬠
Monument to the former site of Qiyuan tea house of
Xi'an Information Office of the Communist Party of China

曾设交通联络站奇园茶社的莲湖公园 ⬠
Lianhu Park, which once set up a traffic Liaison Station of Qiyuan tea house

西北人民革命大学从 1949 年 6 月 25 日正式成立，到 1953 年 6 月改组为西北政法干部学校，学校主要任务是以思想政治教育为主，对学员进行马列主义、毛泽东思想的基础理论知识教育与爱国主义教育。1951 年 12 月 7 日，习仲勋在西北区、陕西省、西安市三级党员干部大会上的报告中说："西北人民革命大学的办法是在绝大多数学校必须大大提倡的办法。"

Northwest People's Revolutionary University was formally established on June 25, 1949, and reorganized into Northwest Political and Legal Cadre School in June 1953. The main task of the school is to give priority to ideological and political education, and to educate students with the basic theoretical knowledge of Marxism-Leninism and Mao Zedong Thought and patriotism. On December 7, 1951, Xi Zhongxun said in his report at the three-level party members and cadres meeting from Northwest China, from Shaanxi Province and from Xi'an respectively: "The method of Northwest People's Revolutionary University is a method that must be greatly advocated in most schools."

西北人民革命大学旧址博物馆 ▼
Northwest People's Revolutionary University Site Museum

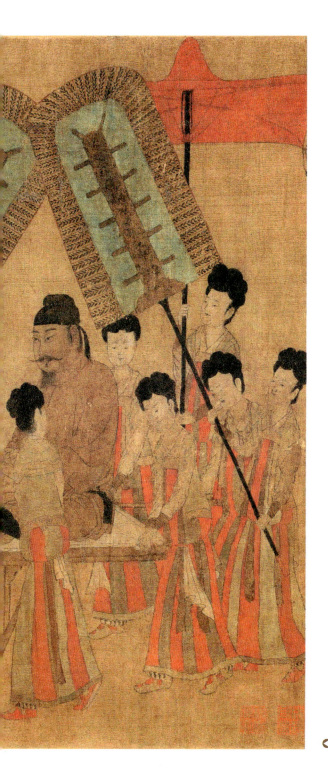

一城文化　婀娜璀璨

卷三

CHAPTER THREE A CITY FEATURED WITH GRACEFUL AND BRILLIANT CULTURE

［唐］阎立本《步辇图》

Emperor on a Sedan Chair of Yan Liben in Tang Dynasty

西安是中国文学最重要的根脉城市之一。中国第一部诗歌总集《诗经》诞生在西安，汉代体物浏亮的赋诞生在西安，古典诗歌的顶峰唐诗在西安，古典小说的代表唐传奇经典在西安，当代文学陕军也在西安。中国艺术的发展基调在西安奠定，从绘画书法、音乐舞蹈到戏剧电影，所有艺术门类都在西安能寻找到其发展的脉络，历久弥新。

浓厚的文化艺术氛围孕育出西安"得天下英才而育之"的独特科教中心气质。西安的综合科教实力居全国城市前列，拥有创新驱动发展的先天优势。

● 西安唐墓乐舞壁画
Emperor on a Sedan Chair

Xi'an is one of the most important root cities of Chinese literature. *The Book of Songs*, China's first collection of poems, was born in Xi'an, while fu, the descriptive rhymed prose with clear subject matters in Han Dynasty, was also born here. The peak of classical poetry is Tang poetry in Xi'an, the representative of classical novels is Tang legend classics in Xi'an, and the Shaanxi Writers Group of contemporary literature is also found in Xi'an. The keynote of the development of Chinese art is established in Xi'an. From painting and calligraphy, music and dance to dramas and films, all kinds of art can find their development veins in Xi'an, lasting and thriving.

The strong cultural and artistic atmosphere has bred Xi'an's unique temperament of "educating talents from all over the world" as a scientific and educational center. Xi'an ranks among the top cities in China in terms of comprehensive scientific and educational strength, and has the inherent advantage of innovation-driven development.

人间风流是诗乡
Cradle of Chinese Poetry and Prose

西安是中国文学的故乡，周代《诗经》、两汉文学、唐诗都在这座城市诞生，并走向巅峰。

Xi'an is the hometown of Chinese literature. *The Book of Songs* of Zhou Dynasty, the literature of Han Dynasty and Tang poetry were born in this city and reached their peaks.

《诗经》与西安

The Book of Songs and Xi'an

中国诗歌、中国文学的源头——《诗经》，完成总编纂于此，四分之三的篇章同西安密切相关。《诗经》代表着中国文化天真烂漫的时代，"不学诗，无以言"。

《诗经》传为西周宣王时期大臣尹吉甫采集，历经孔子编订，毛苌、毛亨的弘扬，西汉时被尊为儒家经典，始称《诗经》，并沿用至今。

诗经在内容上分为《风》《雅》《颂》三个部分。《风》是周代各地的歌谣；《雅》是周人的正声雅乐，又分《小雅》和《大雅》；《颂》是周王庭和贵族宗庙祭祀的乐歌。《诗经》有诸多的名句流传至今，如《蒹葭》咏唱的："蒹葭苍苍，白露为霜。所谓伊人，在水一方。"《采薇》的"昔我往矣，杨柳依依，今我来思，雨雪霏霏"等。

The Book of Songs, the source of Chinese poetry and literature, has been compiled here, and three quarters of its chapters are closely related to Xi'an. The Book of Songs represents the naive era of Chinese culture: "If you don't learn poetry, you can't say anything".

The Book of Songs was compiled by Yin Jifu, Minister of King Xuanwang in Western Zhou, edited by Confucius and promoted by Mao Chang and Mao Heng. It was regarded as a Confucian classic in Western Han Dynasty, when it was for the first time entitled The Book of Songs which is still in use today.

The Book of Songs is divided into three parts in content: Feng, Ya and Song. "Feng" (custom) is a collection of ballads or folk songs from all over Zhou Dynasty. "Ya" (elegance) is a collection of the positive and elegant voices of Zhou people, which is divided into "Xiaoya" (minor elegance) and "Daya" (major elegance). "Song" (ode) is a number of musical songs for the court and the nobles' ancestral temple sacrifices. There are many famous lines in The Book of Songs that have been passed down to this day, for example, "The reeds by the river are green and pale, and the dew is frosted in autumn. Where is my love? On the other side of the river " in "The Reeds", and "Think of the day when I first left home for the troops, the willows were billowing in the spring breeze, but now on the way back, heavy snow is falling from all over the sky" in "Collecting Seedlings".

诗三百，一言以蔽之，曰思无邪。

——《论语·为政第二》（节选）

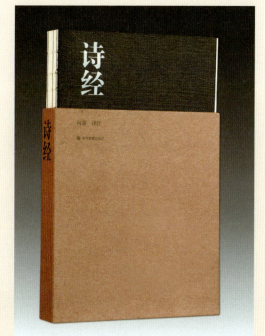

《诗经》
Book of Songs

两汉文学在西安

Literature in Western and Eastern Han Dynasties

大风起分云飞扬，安得猛士分守四方。

——【西汉】刘邦《大风歌》（节选）

与雄浑壮烈的大汉盛世相契，汉朝的文学空前繁荣。

汉赋作为汉代的文学形式，极尽文辞之华美、感情之澎湃、想象之雄奇。在两汉的400余年中，大批的文人以超凡的想象，展示了东方语言的韵律之美。汉赋兼收并蓄《诗经》、楚辞、先秦散文等诸种文体，形成了一种容量宏大、铺张扬厉的综合型文学样式。其中，班固的《两都赋》、张衡的《两京赋》都为汉大赋力作，极力描写了长安城的繁华，表现都城的壮丽宏大，宫殿的奇伟华美。更有贾谊的骚体赋《吊屈原赋》和枚乘的《七发》标志汉大赋正式形成，司马相如的大赋成为汉赋顶峰。

The literature of Han Dynasty was unprecedentedly flourishing, which coincided with the vigorous Han Dynasty's prosperity.

Han fu, as a literary form in Han Dynasty, is extremely rich in rhetoric, emotion and imagination. During the 400 years of Han Dynasty, a large number of scholars showed us the beauty of the rhythm of the eastern language with extraordinary imagination. Han fu incorporates literary styles of diverse nature, including *The Book of Songs*, "Chu Ci" (poetry of Chu State), Pre-Qin (Dynasty) prose and so on. Among them, Ban Gu's "*Ode to the Two Capitals*" and Zhang Heng's "*Ode to the Two Capitals*" are masterpieces of Han fu, i.e. rhymed descriptive prose interspersed with verse in Han Dynasty, which describe the prosperity of Chang'an City and show the grandeur of the capital and the splendor of its palaces. Moreover, Jia Yi's Li Sao-styled fu, "*Mourning for Qu Yuan*" and Mei Sheng's "*Qifa*" (seven statements) marked the formal formation of Han fu, and Sima Xiangru's Dafu became the peak of this special kind of prose written in Han Dynasty.

《上林赋》 ❂
"Ode to Shanglin Royal Garden"

史家之绝唱，无韵之离骚。
——鲁迅

成书于长安的《史记》开创了中国纪传体史书的先河，被公认为中国史书典范，还因其在文学上的巨大成就，被鲁迅先生誉为"史家之绝唱，无韵之《离骚》"。其作者司马迁（前145—？），生于夏阳（今陕西省韩城市），是汉朝最伟大的史学家。因替投降匈奴的李陵求情，司马迁被处以宫刑，开始在狱中写《史记》。出狱后在长安任中书令，继续写作。

Records of the Historian, completed in Chang'an, initiated the the style of history presented in a series of biographies in China, and has ever since been recognized as a model of Chinese history books. Because of its great achievements in literature, it was praised by Lu Xun as "the masterpiece for all historians, and another *Li Sao without rhyme*". The author Sima Qian (145 B.C. -), born in Xiayang (now Hancheng, Shaanxi Province), is the greatest historian in Han Dynasty. Sima Qian was sentenced to castration for pleading for Li Ling who had surrendered to the Huns, the nomad tribe in the north, and began to write *Records of the Historian* in prison. After he was released from prison, he served as head of the secretariat in Chang'an and continued his writing.

◀ 《史记》
Records of the Historian

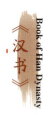

　　《汉书》是继《史记》之后的又一部卓越的历史与文学著作，它开创了"包举一代"的断代史体例，成为后世修史的范本。刘知几评价《汉书》"自尔迄今，无改斯道"，可见其史学地位之重要。作者班固（32—92）扶风安陵（今陕西咸阳东北）人。

　　Book of Han Dynasty is another outstanding historical and literary work after *Records of the Historian*, which initiated the dynastic history style of "covering the history of a whole generation" and became a model for later generations to chronicle the history. Liu Zhiji's evaluation of *Book of Han Dynasty*, "Since then, there has been no change in the way", shows its important historical position. The author Ban Gu (32-92) was born in Anling, Fufeng (now northeast of Xianyang, Shaanxi Province).

自尔迄今，无改斯道。

——【唐】刘知几《史通》（节选）

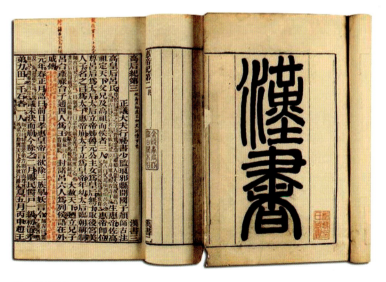

🔶 《汉书》
Book of Han Dynasty

长安一片月，万户捣衣声。

——【唐】李白

《子夜吴歌·秋歌》（节选）

唐代是中国古典诗歌的最高峰，盛世长安则是唐代最杰出诗人与作品的汇集地，长安是中国文学的沃土，是中国诗歌的沃土，也是中国文人的文心所在。唐代文人以诗篇为后人展现盛唐时期自信、骄傲而立体的长安诗魂。

"诗仙"李白三入长安，并为这片土地写下"长相思，在长安""云想衣裳花想容"等名句；"诗圣"杜甫在长安少陵原生活十年，因此自号"少陵野老"；隐居在辋川别业中的"诗佛"王维所著《辋川集》可谓是长安田园风光的最佳代言。

Chinese classical poetry reached its summit in Tang Dynasty, and Chang'an was then the gathering place of the most outstanding poets and works. Chang'an was the fertile soil of Chinese literature and Chinese poetry, where the literary heart of Chinese writers resided. Scholars in Tang Dynasty used poems to present the confident, proud and three-dimensional poetic soul of Chang'an in the prosperous Tang Dynasty.

Li Bai, a "poet-immortal", entered Chang'an three times, and wrote famous lines such as "No wonder the white clouds and peonies are so eager to dress up for you". Du Fu, lived in Chang'an for ten years, so he called himself "Wild Old Man of Shaoling". *Wangchuan Collection* written by Wang Wei, a "poet-Buddha", who lived in seclusion in Wangchuan, could be considered the best endorsement of Chang'an pastoral scenery.

"曲江赴宴"和"雁塔题名"是当时士子炫耀功名之莫上荣光，被誉为"天地间第一流人第一等事也"。大诗人白居易进士及第后，便在塔壁留诗"慈恩塔下题名处，十七人中最少年"。白居易喜欢平易近人的诗风，以让黄发垂髫皆能背诵为乐。在长安鳌屋（西安周至县）担任县尉时，他写下了"天长地久有时尽，此恨绵绵无绝期"的哀婉诗篇。

　　"Attending Qujiang banquet" and "inscribing names on Wild Goose Pagoda" were the glory for scholars to flaunt their scholarly honors or official ranks at that time, and were hailed as "the first-rate matter for the first-rate people in the world". Bai Juyi, a great poet, after passing the imperial examination, left these lines on the tower wall, "Among people whose names are inscribed, I am the youngest of the seventeen". Bai Juyi preferred the approachable poetic style, hoping that both the young and the old could recite his poems for fun. When he was a county commandant in Chang'an (Zhouzhi County, Xi'an), he wrote a long pathetic poem "Song of Everlasting Sorrow", which includes these memerable lines: "Long as the heaven and the earth are, there would always be an end, but this remorse of life and death could certainly last without an end."

唐阎林侠事李白
Portrait of Li bai

杜工部
Portrait of Du Fu

韩愈和贾岛的"推敲"典故就发生在长安大街之上。韩愈开创以文入诗之先河，被尊为"唐宋八大家"之首。"云横秦岭家何在，雪拥蓝关马不前"，正是这位大文豪离开长安时的思绪哀愁。

　　更有生于长安、长于长安，死后更是归葬长安少陵原的柳宗元；常居长安城南樊川的杜牧；赞叹着"蓝田日暖玉生烟"的李商隐……

　　Han Yu and Jia Dao's "push or knock" allusion took place on one of the Chang'an streets. Han Yu pioneered the introduction of prose style into poetry, and was honored as the first of the "Eight Masters of Tang and Song Dynasties". "The clouds hovering the Qinling Mountains, where is my home? The snow holding the blue horse back, what can I do?" are lines that express his sorrow of leaving the city of Chang'an.

　　More famous writers were once here in Chan'an. Liu Zongyuan was born, grew up, died and was even buried in Shaolingyuan, Chang'an. Du Mu long lived in Fanchuan, south of Chang'an. Li Shangyin exclaimed beauty of Chang'an by writing these lines, "The sun in Lantian is shining warm, so the light mist rises from the hills of jade"...

● 【明】仇英《辋川十景图卷》（部分）
Book of Han Dynasty painting by QiuYing in Ming Dynasty

唐代传奇标志着中国古代小说进入了一个新的创作阶段。其中优秀代表性作品有元稹的《莺莺传》，白行简的《李娃传》，陈鸿的《长恨歌传》，李朝威的《柳毅传》，蒋防的《霍小玉传》等。

白行简以长安为背景创作的作品——《李娃传》（又称《汧国夫人传》）与唐诗一样被誉为"一代之奇"，是中国小说进入成熟阶段的唐传奇的代表作之一。其名篇有《天地阴阳交欢大乐赋》，荷兰汉学家高罗佩对全文的评语为："这篇文章文风优美，提供了许多关于唐代的生活习惯的材料。"

The emergence of legends in Dynasty marks that the creation of ancient Chinese novels has entered a new stage. Among them are Yuan Zhen's *Biography of Yingying*, Bai Xingjian's *Biography of Li Wa*, Chen Hong's *Biography of Everlasting Sorrow*, Li Chaowei's *Biography of Liu Yi*, Jiang Fang's Biography of Huo Xiaoyu and so on.

Bai Xingjian's work, *Biography of Li Wa* (also known as *Biography of the Lady of Qian State*), which is set in Chang'an, is known as "the wonder of a generation" like Tang poetry, and is one of the representative works of Tang legends when Chinese novels enter into a mature stage. His famous article is "*Ode to the Harmonious Joy of Heaven, Earth, Yin and Yang*". The Dutch sinologist Robert Hans van Gulik (Chinese name Gao Luopei) commented on the full text, saying "This article has a beautiful style and provides a lot of information about the living habits of Tang Dynasty."

小说亦如诗，至唐代而一变。
——鲁迅《中国小说史略》（节选）

琳琅满目画韵长
Dazzling Array of Beautiful Paintings

从远古的半坡时期到周秦汉唐，西安传承并保留着多样态的绘画艺术形式，有奠定中国绘画发展基础的史前彩陶纹饰艺术、创造中国古典美术发展巅峰的汉代美术作品群、中国古代壁画的集大成者——唐代壁画，更是产生了如吴道子、阎立本、阎立德等一大批闻名中外的画家。

From the ancient Banpo period to Zhou, Qin, Han and Tang Dynasties, Xi'an has inherited and retained various painting art forms, including prehistoric painted pottery decoration art which laid the foundation for the development of Chinese painting, Han Dynasty art works which created the peak of Chinese classical art development, and Tang Dynasty frescoes, an epitome of all ancient Chinese frescoes. In additon, it has produced a large number of painters famous at home and abroad, such as Wu Daozi, Yan Liben and Yan Lide.

懿德太子墓壁画《阙楼图》 ▶
Mural of Prince Yide's tomb *Watchtower*

章怀太子墓壁画《客使图》 ●
Mural of Prince Zhanghuai's tomb *Foreign Envoys*

中国古代壁画集大成者非隋唐时代的长安墓葬壁画莫属。由于唐代兼容并蓄的文化风格，唐墓葬壁画吸收了许多其他民族的文化特点。陪葬乾陵的唐懿德太子墓、永泰公主墓和章怀太子墓墓葬规模空前，壁画精美程度也都令人叹为观止。懿德太子墓的《阙楼图》气象宏大，威仪壮观，配以浩浩荡荡的《仪仗图》，体现了大唐帝国的强盛和威严；章怀太子墓的《客使图》《观鸟捕蝉图》形神兼备，是公认的唐代水平最高的人物画作品；新城长公主墓的仕女壁画画风细腻，色彩鲜明，个性突出，也是不可多得的唐代壁画精品。

The epitome of ancient Chinese frescoes is absolutely Chang'an tomb frescoes in Sui and Tang Dynasties. Due to the inclusive cultural style of Tang Dynasty, the frescoes of Tang tombs absorbed the cultural characteristics of many nationalities. The tombs of Prince Yide, Princess Yongtai and Prince Zhanghuai, which are affiliated to Qianling Mausoleum, are unprecedented in scale and amazing with the exquisite frescoes. Inside Prince Yide's tomb, the magnificent and dignified fresco of "*Watchtower*", accompanied by the mighty fresco of "*Ceremonial Procession*", reflects the prosperity and majesty of the Great Tang Empire. Inside Prince Zhanghuai's tomb, the frescoes of "*Guests and Envoys*" and "*Watching Birds Catching Cicadas*", are recognized as the highest level figure paintings of Tang Dynasty. And the frescoes of Princess Royal's Tomb in Xincheng are exquisite in style, bright in color and outstanding in character, which are also rare fine frescoes from Tang Dynasty.

唐代绘画
Paintings of Tang Dynasty

　　长安的山水画以王维的作品为代表，他的山水画集众家之妙，以单纯的水墨变化表达淡雅的景色和心境。对中国的山水画产生了深远的影响。

　　唐代著录中计有花鸟画家八十多人，如薛稷画鹤，韩干画马，韩滉、韦偃画牛，李泓画虎，卢弁画猫，张旻画鸡，齐旻画犬，李逖画昆虫，张立画竹，等等。现在留存于世的著名唐代花鸟画有薛稷的《顾步鹤图》《啄苔鹤图》，以及韩滉的《五牛图》等。

　　唐代人物画中最杰出的代表莫过于张萱的《虢国夫人游春图》《捣练图》，周昉的《簪花仕女图》《挥扇仕女图》，吴道子的《送子天王图》《八十七神仙卷》《地狱变相图》等。阎立本所绘人物形象逼真，有《步辇图》《凌烟阁二十四功臣图》《秦府十八学士图》等大型人物画卷。阎立本兄阎立德在艺术上与其齐名，曾奉诏画《王会图》，还画过《文成公主降番图》。

Chang'an landscape paintings are represented by Wang Wei's works. His landscape paintings integrate the best of many paingting styles, and express elegant sceneries and quiet moods with simple ink changes. It has a profound influence on Chinese landscape painting.

In Tang Dynasty, there were more than 80 flower and bird painters, such as Xue Ji painting cranes, Han Gan painting horses, Han Huang and Wei Yan painting cattle, Li Hong painting tigers, Lu Bian painting cats, Zhang Min painting chickens, Qi Min painting dogs, Li Ti painting insects, Zhang Li painting bamboos and so on. Famous flower-and-bird paintings in Tang Dynasty that are still available today include Xue Ji's "*Watching Strolling Cranes*" and "*Cranes Pecking on Mosses*", and Han Huang's "*Penta-Bull Painting*", etc.

The most outstanding representatives of Tang Dynasty figure paintings are Zhang Xuan's "*Lady Guo on a Spring Outing*" and "*Tamping Boiled Silk*", Zhou Fang's "*Ladies Wearing Hairpins*" and "*Fan-swinging Ladies*", Wu Daozi's "*Baby-delivering God of Heaven*", "*Eighty-seven Immortals*" and "*Tortures in the Hell*", and so on. The vivd portrayal of characters can be seen in Yan Liben's paintings of "*Emperor on a Sedan Chair*", "*Twenty-four Heroes of Lingyan Pavilion*" and "*Eighteen Scholars of Qin House*". Yan Lide is as famous as Yan Liben, his younger brother, in art. He once painted "*Emperor Meeting Foreign Envoys in Court*" by follwing the emperor's decree and also "*Princess Wencheng Married to Tubo*".

千载风华墨痕香
Enjoying Wonderful Calligraphy Art on Steles

唐代书法是整个中国书法发展史的高峰，无论是书家、书体、风格流派，还是书法理论，都达到了前所未有的高度，书法名家辈出，且多集中于长安。这一时期的杰出代表颜真卿、张旭、怀素、柳公权等一代大家们更以其独特的艺术魅力成为后世楷模，开启唐代书法之盛事。书法与碑刻密不可分，碑林成为书法爱好者的天堂。

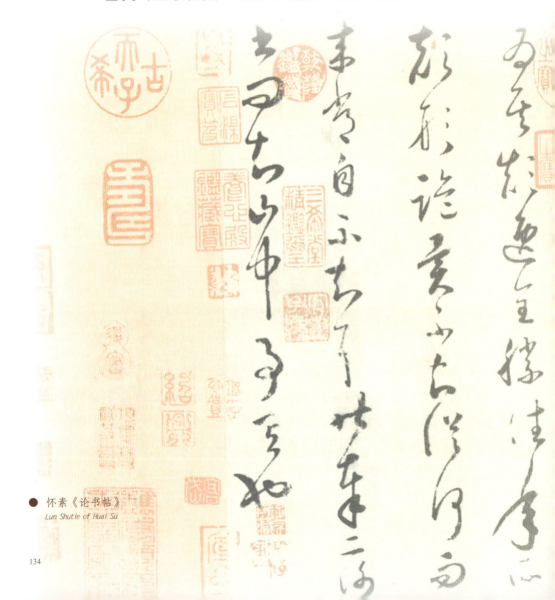

● 怀素《论书帖》
Lun Shutie of Huai Su

The calligraphy of Tang Dynasty has reached an unprecedented height in the whole history of Chinese calligraphy, whether it be calligraphers, writing styles, genres or calligraphy theory. Famous calligraphers came forth in large numbers, and most of them assembled in Chang'an. The outstanding representatives of this period, such as Yan Zhenqing, Zhang Xu, Huai Su and Liu Gongquan, with their unique artistic charm, have become the models for later generations, which can be considered the great event of calligraphy in Tang Dynasty. Calligraphy and inscription are inseparable, and the forest of steles has become a paradise for calligraphy enthusiasts.

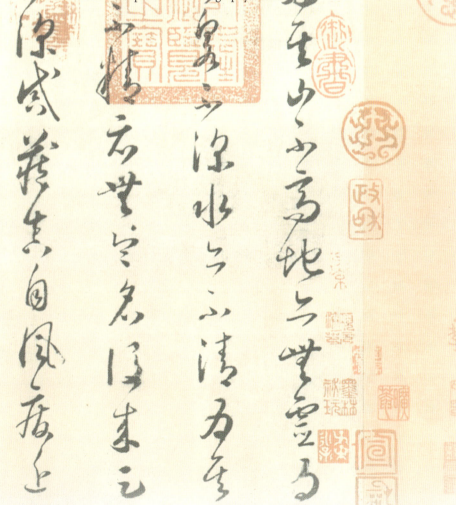

碑林位于西安市文昌门内三学街，1944 年建立博物馆，1993 年 1 月改名西安碑林博物馆。其是利用西安孔庙古建筑群扩建而成的一座以收藏、研究和陈列历代碑石、墓志及石刻造像为主的艺术博物馆，也是陕西创建最早的博物馆。馆区由孔庙、碑林、石刻艺术室三部分组成，现有馆藏文物 11000 余件。陈列由碑林、石刻艺术和其他文物展览三部分组成，共 12 个展室。碑林博物馆集中展藏古代碑石墓志时间最早、拥有名碑最多，被公认为"世界最古老的石刻书库"。碑林博物馆不仅是中国古代文化典籍刻石的聚集之地，也是历代著名书法艺术珍品的荟萃之地，被誉为"书法之渊、经史之薮"。

西安碑林博物馆
Xi'an Beilin Museum

Located in Sanxue Street inside Wenchang Gate, Xi'an, the museum was established in 1944 and renamed Xi'an Beilin Museum in January 1993. It is an art museum expanded from the ancient Confucius Temple complex, which mainly collects, studies and exhibits steles, epitaphs and stone carvings of past dynasties. It is also the earliest museum established in Shaanxi. The museum is composed of Confucius Temple, Forest of Steles and Stone Carving Art Room, with a total collection of more than 11,000 cultural relics. The exhibition consists of three parts: the forest of steles, stone carving art and other cultural relic exhibitions, totalling 12 exhibition rooms. The museum is the earliest museum to intensively collect steles and epitaphs of ancient times and posseses the largest number of famous steles, so it is recognized as the "stack room of the oldest stone carvings in the world". The museum is a gathering place not only for stone carvings of ancient Chinese classics, but also for famous calligraphy art treasures of past dynasties, which is known as "the origin of calligraphy and the source of classics".

碑林石台孝经亭 ▼
Stone-based Pavilion for Filial Piety Classic in Beilin Museum

《开成石经》现藏于西安碑林博物馆，国宝级文物，是唐代的十二经刻石，又称唐石经。原碑立于唐长安城务本坊的国子监内，宋时移至府学北墉，即今西安碑林。中国清代以前所刻石经很多，唯《开成石经》保存最为完好，是研究中国经书历史的重要资料。

唐文宗太和四年（830），时任工部侍郎兼充翰林侍讲学士的郑覃，向唐文宗进言："请召宿儒奥学，校定六籍，准后汉故事，勒石于太学，永代作则，以正其阙。"请求将儒学经典刊刻于石碑，立于太学。太和七年（833）12月，项目正式启动，开成二年（837）9月，这一中国文化史上最为宏大的工程正式竣工，因开成年间刻成，后人称为《开成石经》，距今已有1180余年。

Kaicheng Stone Classics is now a national treasure in the collection of Xi'an Forest of Steles Museum. It is a stone carved with Twelve Confucian Classics of Tang Dynasty, also known as Tang Stone Classics. The original stone tablet first stood in the imperial academy located at Wubenfang in Chang'an City of Tang Dynasty, and later moved to government-run school, Beiyong, in Song Dynasty, which is now the site of Xi'an Forest of Steles Museum. Before Qing Dynasty, there were many stone classic carvings in China, but Kaicheng Stone Classics is the best preserved, and an important material for studying the history of Chinese classics.

In the fourth year of Taihe Period of Emperor Wenzong (830), Zheng Qin, then assistant minister of the Ministry of Works and a scholar of the Imperial Academy, made a suggestion to Emperor Wenzong, "Please invite some most learned Confucian scholars to proofread the six classics, to confirm the historical records of Later Han, and to carve them on stones at the Imperial College. In this way, they will set a model for following generations so as to correct their mistakes." And it was accepted by the Emperor. In December of the 7th year of Taihe Period (833), the project was officially started, and in September of the 2nd year of Kaicheng Period (837), the grandest project in Chinese cultural history was officially completed. It was called Kaicheng Stone Classics by later generations, and it has been about 1,180 years since.

　　《大秦景教流行中国碑》现藏于西安碑林博物馆，国宝级文物，入选中央电视台《国家宝藏》节目。唐《大秦景教流行中国碑》由景教传教士伊斯出资、景净撰述、吕秀岩书刻，于唐建中二年（781）在长安大秦寺落成，唐后期被埋入地下，明天启年间在西安西郊（一说周至县）出土。保存完好，字迹清晰，书法秀丽，史料价值极高，是研究景教历史及其在中国唐代传播的情况，中国古代与叙利亚、伊朗等地文化交流、友好往来的重要实物资料，也是世界考古发现史上最负盛名的"四大石碑"之一。

　　The Nestorian Stele is now a national treasure in the Forest of Steles Museum in Xi'an, and has been selected into the CCTV "National Treasure" program. The stele of Nestorianism spreading in China in Tang Dynasty was funded by Nestorian missionary Isse, written by Jing Jing and engraved by Lü Xiuyan. It was completed in Chang'an Daqin Temple in the second year of Jianzhong Period (781), buried underground in the late Tang Dynasty, and unearthed in the western suburb of Xi'an (Zhouzhi County) in Tianqi Period of Ming Dynasty. It is well preserved, with clear handwriting, beautiful calligraphy and extremely high historical value. It is an important material for studying Nestorianism history and its spread in Tang Dynasty of China, as well as cultural exchanges and friendly communications between ancient China and Syria, Iran and other places. It is also one of the most famous "four stone steles" in the history of archaeological discovery in the world.

《大秦景教流行中国碑》拓片
Inscription Rubbing of the Nestorian Stele

格物致知有妙方
Wonderful Recipes for Knowing the Nature of Things

  格物致知的科学技术在西安这座城也取得了辉煌成就。孙思邈、僧一行、李淳风等人代表了中国古代科学技术的最高成就。

  Brilliant achievements have been made in Xi'an in terms of science and technology to know the nature of things. Sun Simiao, Monk Yixing, Li Chunfeng and others represented the people with highest achievements in ancient Chinese science and technology.

● 《耀州华原妙应真人祠记碑》拓片
Inscription Rubbing of Monk Miaoying's Temple Tablet at Huayuan, Yaozhou

孙思邈（541— 682，存在争议），京兆华原（今陕西省铜川市耀州区）人， 唐代医药学家、道士，被后人尊称为"药王"。

孙思邈出生于一个贫穷农民的家庭。他从小就被称为"圣童"，长大后爱好道家老庄学说，隋开皇元年（581），见国事多端，孙思邈隐居陕西终南山，十分重视民间的医疗经验，不断积累走访，及时记录下来，终于完成了他的著作《千金要方》。

Sun Simiao (541-682, controversial), born in Huayuan, Jingzhao (now Yaozhou District, Tongchuan City, Shaanxi Province), is a medical scientist and Taoist priest in Tang Dynasty, and has been honored as the "King of Medicine" by later generations.

Sun Simiao was born into a poor peasant family. He was called a "holy kid" since he was a child. When he grew up, he loved Taoist doctrines. In the first year of Kaihuang Period of Sui Dynasty (581), Sun Simiao lived in the Zhongnans mountains, Shaanxi Province. He attached great importance to folk medical experiences, so he made frequent visits to local experts, collected effective prescriptions and recorded them right away, and finally finished his book *Invaluable Prescriptions for Ready Reference*.

思邈作《千金前方》时已百馀岁，妙尽古今方书之要。

——【宋】叶梦得《避暑录话》（节选）

李淳风（602—670），岐州雍县人，曾在长安为官多年。唐代著名的天文学家、数学家、易学家，精通天文、历算、阴阳之说。

李淳风于贞观七年（633）制成新浑天仪，此仪黄道经纬、赤道经纬、地平经纬均可测定。

唐高宗显庆元年（656），李淳风负责审定并注释《十部算经》，后颁行于国子监。这部算经是世界上最早的算学教材，在中国、日本和朝鲜的学校中沿用多年，且是考核技术官吏的一部重要书籍。闻名中外的计算球体体积的"祖暅定律"就是李淳风注释《九章算术》时，介绍传播的。

李淳风更是世界上第一个给风定级的人。他的名著《乙巳占》重将风划分为八级，是世界气象史上最早的专著。

他和袁天罡还被传说为谶纬学名著《推背图》的作者。因此，英国·李约瑟博士称赞李淳风大概是整个中国历史上最伟大的数学著作注释家。

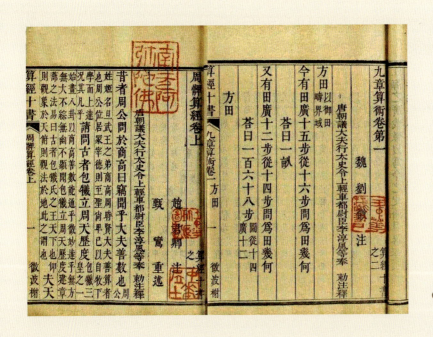

《九章算术》

Nine Chapters on Arithmetic

Li Chunfeng (602-670), a native of Yong County, Qizhou. He served as an official in Chang'an for many years. A famous astronomer, mathematician and expert on Book of Changes in Tang Dynasty, he was proficient in astronomy, calendar calculation and the theory of Yin and Yang.

Li Chunfeng made a new armillary sphere in the 7th year of Zhenguan Period (633), which could measure the longitude and latitude of the ecliptic, equator and horizon.

In the first year of Xianqing Period of Emperor Gaozong (656), Li Chunfeng was responsible for examining and annotating *Ten Calculation Classics*, which was promulgated in the imperial academy. This book is the earliest mathematics textbook in the world. It has been used in schools in China, Japan and Korea for many years, and it is an important book for assessing technical officials. The well-known "Zu Xuan's Law" for calculating the volume of a spheroid was introduced and spread by Li Chunfeng when he annotated *Nine Chapters on Arithmetic*.

Li Chunfeng is the first person in the world to grade the wind. His famous book *Yisi Divining*, which is the earliest monograph in the world meteorological history, divides the wind into eight grades.

He and Yuan Tiangang are also said to be the authors of the famous book "*Push Back Diagram*". Therefore, Dr. Joseph Needham praised Li Chunfeng as probably the greatest annotator of mathematical works in Chinese history.

一行（673—727），唐朝著名天文学家和佛学家，长期在长安大兴善寺中修持。

一行一生中最主要的成就是编制《大衍历》，从开元十七年（729）起，根据《大衍历》编算成的每年的历书颁行全国。经过检验，《大衍历》比唐代已有的其他历法都更精密。开元二十一年（733）传入日本，使用近百年时间。一行在《大衍历》"步晷漏术"中就建立了一个从0度到80度的每度影长与太阳天顶距对应数表，这更是世界数学史上最早的一张正切函数表。

一行受诏改历后曾经组织发起了一次大规模的天文大地测量工作。这次测量，用实测数据彻底地否定了历史上的"日影一寸，地差千里"的错误理论，提供了相当精确的地球子午线一度弧的长度。

一行因获得天文钟的发明权而永垂史册。英国著名科技史家李约瑟博士在《中国科学技术史》第四卷中说，高僧一行所发明的平行联动装置，实质上就是最早的机械时钟，是一切擒纵器的祖先，走在欧洲14世纪第一具机械时钟的前面。

Monk Yixing (673-727), a famous astronomer and Buddhism scholar in Tang Dynasty, practiced Budhist doctrines in Daxingshan Temple in Chang'an for a long time.

His most important achievement in his life is the compilation of *Dayan Calendar*. Since the 17th year of Kaiyuan Period (729), the annual almanac compiled according to *Dayan Calendar* was issued nationwide. After verification, *Dayan Calendar* was more precise than other calendars in Tang Dynasty. In the 21st year of Kaiyuan Period (733), it was introduced into Japan and used for nearly a hundred years. Yixing has set up a numerical table corresponding to the zenith distance of the sun from 0 degrees to 80 degrees in "Shadow Measurement Method" in *Dayan Calendar*, which is the earliest tangent function table in the history of mathematics in the world.

After changing the calendar according the emperor's order, Monk Yixing organized and launched a large-scale astronomical geodetic survey. In this survey, the wrong theory of "an inch of shadow of the sun is a thousand li in distance" was completely negated by the measured data, and the very accurate length of the first arc of the earth meridian was provided.

Monk Yixing is recorded in history because he also invents the astronomical clock. Dr Joseph Needham, a famous British historian of science and technology, said in the fourth volume of *History of Science and Technology in China* that the parallel linkage device invented by Monk Yixing was essentially the earliest mechanical clock, the ancestor of all escapments, and walked ahead of the first mechanical clock in Europe in the 14th century.

僧一行
Monk Yixing

长安三千金世界
Holy Land of Buddhism

　　长安是佛教的圣地，佛教八宗中六家开宗于斯，祖庭林立，高僧辈出。

　　大慈恩寺是中国佛教法相宗（也称"唯识宗""慈恩宗"）祖庭之一，唐长安三大译经场之一，是唐长安城内知名度最高、最宏伟瑰丽的佛寺。玄奘曾在此领管佛经译场，其门人窥基于此创立了汉传佛教八大宗派之一的法相宗。

　　净业寺位于西安市长安区终南山北麓，是中国"佛教八宗"之一律宗的祖庭。净业寺建于隋朝，唐初为高僧道宣法师的弘法道场。

　　大兴善寺是中国佛教密宗祖庭、著名的隋唐皇家寺院、隋朝第一所国立译经馆、唐长安三大译经场之一。著名的成语"醍醐灌顶"一词的"灌顶"，就是大兴善寺首开。

● 净业寺山门
Gate to Jingye Temple

Chang'an is a holy land of Buddhism, and six of the eight Buddhism sects are settled here in this city, with numerous ancestral courts and numerous eminent monks.

Da Ci'en Temple is one of the ancestral courts of Faxiang Sect (also known as "Consciousness First Sect" and "Ci'en Sect") of Chinese Buddhism, one of the three major scripture translation sites and the most famous and magnificent Buddhist temple in Chang'an in Tang Dynasty. Eminent Monk Xuanzang once took charge of the Buddhist scripture translation here, and his disciple Kuiji therein founded Faxiang Sect, one of the eight sects of the Han Buddhism.

Jingye Temple is located at the northern foot of Mount Zhongnan in Chang'an District, Xi'an. It is the ancestral court of Vinaya Sect, one of the eight Buddhist sects in China. Jingye Temple was built in Sui Dynasty, and it was the monastery of preaching the dharma by the eminent monk Daoxuan in the early Tang Dynasty.

Da Xingshan Temple is one of the ancestral temples of Chinese Buddhism, the famous royal temple of Sui and Tang Dynasties, the first national translation site of Sui Dynasty, and one of the three translation sites of Chang'an in Tang Dynasty. The famous Chinese idiom "a sudden surge of awakening" finds its origin here.

姚秦羅什尊者

草堂寺是中国"佛教八宗"之一——三论宗的祖庭，是中国第一座国立翻译佛经译场，也是佛教三大译场中时间最长、规模最大的译场，是佛教中国化的起点，也是"佛经第一译师"鸠摩罗什译经和存放舍利之所。鸠摩罗什是天才的导师，以"三寸不烂之舌"弘传佛法，唐太宗赞颂当年盛况"十万流沙来振锡，三千弟子共译经"。

华严寺是"佛教八宗"之一华严宗的祖庭，其位于西安南郊长安区韦曲东南少陵原半坡上，现保存有华严初祖杜顺大师和澄观法师的灵骨塔。

香积寺是净土宗祖庭，唐高宗永隆二年（681），净土宗创始人善导大师圆寂，弟子怀恽为纪念其功德，修建灵骨塔、崇灵塔和香积寺。王维的诗歌《过香积寺》曾被选入日本小学课本："不知香积寺，数里入云峰，古木无人径，深山何处钟。泉声咽危石，日色冷青松。薄暮空潭曲，安禅制毒龙。"

草堂寺
Caotang Temple

Caotang Temple is the ancestral court of Sanlun Sect, one of the eight Buddhist sects in China, the first national translation site for Buddhist scriptures in China, the longest and largest translation site among the three major Buddhist translation sites, the starting point for the sinicization of Buddhism, and the place where Kumarajiva, the first translator of Buddhist scriptures, translated Buddhist scriptures and Buddhist relics were preserved. Kumarajiva, a gifted teacher, preached Buddhism with his "eloquent tongue" here, so Emperor Taizong praised the grand occasion by writing these lines, "Tens of thousand of people swarm into the monastery, and tens of hundred of them are translating sutras together".

Huayan Temple, the ancestral court of Huayan Sect, one of the eight Buddhist sects, is located on the half slope of Shaolingyuan, southeast of Weiqu, Chang'an District, in the southern suburb of Xi'an, and now houses the holy bone towers of Master Du Shun, the founder of Huayan Sect, and Master Monk Cheng Guan.

Xiangji temple is the ancestral court of Pure Land Sect. In the second year of Yonglong Period of Emperor Gaozong (681), the founder of Pure Land Sect, Master Monk Shandao died. His disciple Huai Yun built Holy Bone Tower, Chongling Tower and Xiangji temple to commemorate the founder's merits and virtues. Wang Wei's poem *Passing by Xiangji Temple* was selected into Japanese primary school textbook, which reads, "Not knowing the way to the Temple, I wondered miles into the mountains high. Through ancient woods without a human track, I suddenly heard a bell echoing far. A rillet was singing over high rocks, and the sun was shining upon the green pines. The twilight could make noises but ethereal, but could deep meditation conquer all evils? ".

华严寺 ⊙
Huayan Temple

香积寺 ⊙
Xiangji Temple

横渠四句风骨昂
Brilliant Wisdom Conveyed by the Four Do's Aphorisms

　　有宋一代，张载创"关学"，一代文人，气盖江河，让历史为之一颤。关学是理学的主要分支，成为中国儒学的重要流派，其经世致用的特点一直影响着历代的志士仁人。

In Song Dynasty, and great thinker and educator Zhang Zai created "Guan Xue", a Confuscian School of Guanzhong, whose influence is far-reaching and epoch-making. Guan Xue is the main branch of Neo-Confucianism, and it has become an important school of Chinese Confucianism. Its humanistic pragmatism has always influenced people with lofty ideals in all ages.

张载（1020—1077）生于长安，卒于临潼，北宋理学创始人之一。因居于陕西关中，其所创学派又被称为"关学"。由于他是陕西眉县横渠镇人，自号"横渠"，关中学派亦被称为"横渠学派"。

张载曾在长安以及武功绿野书院、扶风贤山寺等地讲学，门徒多为关中地区有识之士和在职官员。"为天地立心，为生民立命，为往圣继绝学，为万世开太平"是张载思想的精髓所在，冯友兰称其为"横渠四句"，为后世传颂。作为宋代理学的主要奠基人之一，张载的关学与濂、洛、闽之学并驾齐驱，自成体系，其思想对后世影响深远。

Zhang Zai (1020-1077), who was born in Chang'an and died in Lintong, is one of the founders of Neo-Confucianism in Northern Song Dynasty. Because he lived in Guanzhong, Shaanxi Province, his school was also called Guan Xue (Guangzhong School). Because he is from Hengqu Town, Meixian County, Shaanxi Province, he is also called "Hengqu", hence the name of "Hengqu School" for his thought.

Zhang Zai delivered lectures in Chang'an, Wugong Luye Academy of Classical Learning and Fufeng Xianshan Temple, and his disciples were mostly people of insight and serving officials in Guanzhong area. The essence of Zhang Zai's thought lies in the popular "Four Do's Aphorisms of Hengqu", a term give by philosopher Feng Youlan, which goes, "to ordain conscience for Heaven and Earth, to secure life and fortune for the people, to continue lost teachings for past sages, and to establish peace for all future generations". As one of the main founders of Neo-Confucianism in Song Dynasty, Zhang Zai's Guan Xue keeps abreast with the studies of Lian, Luo and Min schools while establishing its own system, which has had profound influence on later generations ever since.

诚明所知，乃天德良知，非见闻小知而已。

——【北宋】张载《正蒙·诚明篇》（节选）

◀ 张载像
Portrait of Zhangzai

被誉为全国四大著名书院之一、西北四大书院之冠。

明万历二十年（1592），陕西著名学者、御史冯从吾在此讲学多年，弟子日众。万历三十七年（1609）十月，陕西布政使汪可受等，为冯从吾另择宝庆寺之东小悉园处创建关中书院。书院中建讲堂六楹，题匾名"允执堂"。取自儒学"允执其中"之意。明清时期的关中书院在人才培养方面发挥了很大作用，为关中培育了一批"务戒空谈、敦实行"的儒生。

关中书院与冯从吾的故事，至今令人动容。天启四年（1624），权奸魏忠贤为笼络人心，授冯从吾以南京右都御史、工部尚书等职召用，冯从吾坚辞不就，依旧定期在关中书院讲学。天启五年（1625）秋，魏忠贤党羽张讷上疏诋毁冯从吾，冯从吾被削籍。次年，熹宗在魏忠贤操纵下，下令毁天下书院。冯从吾的同乡、吏部尚书王绍徽曾仿《水浒》故事，编东林党108人为《点将录》，献给魏忠贤，冯从吾亦被列入其内。那时，魏忠贤的党羽乔应甲巡抚陕西，为向其主子谄媚邀功，捣毁了关中书院。冯从吾为此痛之切肤，咯血病榻，含恨而卒。

Guanzhong Academy is known as one of the four most famous academies in China and the top of the four academies in Northwest China.

In the 20th year of Wanli Period in Ming Dynasty (1592), Feng Congwu, a famous scholar and supervisor of Shaanxi Province, delivered lectures here for many years, and his disciples were numerous. In October of the thirty-seventh year of Wanli Period (1609), Wang Keshou, the governor of Shaanxi Province, together with others, founded Guanzhong Academy for Feng Congwu by selecting its site in Xiaoxi Garden on the east of Baoqing Temple. There was a six-room lecture hall in the academy, with the title of "Yun Zhi Tang", which was taken from Confucian classics with the meaning of "being impartial". Guanzhong Academy in Ming and Qing Dynasties played a very important role in personnel training, and cultivated a group of Confucian scholars who were "willing to take actions rather than to do empty talks" for Guanzhong area.

The story of Guanzhong Academy and Feng Congwu is still memorable. In the fourth year of Tianqi Period (1624), the reacherous court official Wei Zhongxian, to win over other people's support, offered Feng Congwu such titles as Imperial Censor of Nanjing and Minister of Works. But Feng rejected these offers and insisted on lecturing regularly at Guanzhong Academy. In the autumn of the fifth year of Tianqi Period (1625), Zhang Ne, a member of Wei Zhongxian gang, slandered Feng Congwu and deprived Feng of his offical ranks. The following year, Emperor Xizong, under the control of Wei Zhongxian, ordered the destruction of all academies in the country. Wang Shaohui, a county fellow of Feng Congwu and an official minister, coined a list of 108 rebels of the Donglin Party by imitating the story in Outlaws of the Marsh, and offered it to Wei Zhongxian, in which Feng Congwu was also included. At that time, Qiao Yingjia, one of Wei Zhongxian's henchmen, went to Shaanxi to flatter his master and take credit, destroying Guanzhong Academy. Feng Congwu was very sad and suffered from hemoptysis on his deathbed, and died with a strong hatred.

全国四大书院之———关中书院 ▼
Guanzhong Academy – one of the four major academies in China

一曲鼓乐动三秦
Drum Music: Living Fossil of Ancient Music

西安鼓乐是迄今为止在中国境内发现并保存最完整的大型民间乐种之一，是中国古代传统音乐的重要遗存，被国际音乐界和史学界誉为"中国古代音乐活化石"，也是国家级非物质文化遗产。

西安鼓乐脱胎于唐代燕乐，后融于宫廷音乐，安史之乱期间随宫廷乐师的流亡而流入民间。现存清乾隆二十八年（1763）西安鼓乐手抄谱珍藏本的谱字与宋代姜夔十七首自度曲所用的谱字基本相同，由此证明这一珍藏本历史久远，是明清以来已渐在全国失传的俗字乐谱。

西安鼓乐现存的一千一百余首曲目中包含了部分与唐代大曲、唐宋燕乐曲、教坊大曲等唐宋音乐同名的曲目，它堪与唐宋大曲相比的庞大结构形式和不容纳明清以来新生乐器的乐队配置，显示出某种原始性特征，反映了西安鼓乐严格继承唐宋音乐的状况。

现在常用的曲目有《鼓段子》《打扎子》《引令》《套词》《南词》《曲破》《杂曲》等。

渔阳鼙鼓动地来，惊破霓裳羽衣曲。

——【唐】白居易《长恨歌》（节选）

Xi'an drum music is one of the most complete large-scale folk music found and preserved in China so far, and it is an important relic of ancient Chinese traditional music. A national intangible cultural heritage, it is praised as "the living fossil of ancient Chinese music" by international musicians and historians.

Xi'an drum music was born out of Yan music in Tang Dynasty, and then merged into court music. During the An-Shi Rebellion, it spread among the ordinary people with the exile of court musicians. The then existing Xi'an drum music hand-written notation characters in the 28th year of Emperor Qianlong's reign in

西安鼓乐 ⬠
Xi'an Drum Music

Qing Dynasty (1763), were basically the same as those used in the seventeen self-performed songs of Jiang Kui in Song Dynasty, which proves that this collection of notation characters had a long history and had been a popular music score until it was gradually lost in the whole country since Ming and Qing Dynasties.

More than 1,100 existing tracks of Xi'an drum music include some tracks with the same names as Tang (dynasty) Daqu, Tang and Song (dynasties) Yan Music, Jiaofang (imperial music office) Daqu and other Tang and Song music pieces. Xi'an drum music can be played with huge structural form of Tang and Song Daqu and with band configuration that does not accommodate new musical instruments since Ming and Qing Dynasties, which shows its primitive characteristics, and can reflect the fact that Xi'an drum music strictly inherits Tang and Song music.

At present, the commonly performed music tracks include "*Gu Duanzi*", "*Da Zhazi*", "*Yin Ling*", "*Tao Ci*", "*Nan Ci*", "*Qu Po*", "*Za Qu*" and so on.

文艺精品世无双
Unrivaled High-quality Literary and Artistic Works

西安被称为"文化之城"，从二十世纪八九十年代的"文学陕军"为中国文学界贡献一批优秀的攻坚力量，到黄土画派、长安画派等绘画领域的大师名作享誉全国，再到影视演艺、戏曲艺术"百花齐放"，西安的文艺精品在中国刮起一股强劲的"西北风"。

Xi'an is known as the "City of Culture". Since the 1980s and 1990s, "Shaanxi Writers Group" has contributed a large number of outstanding people to Chinese literature and art. The famous masterpieces of the artists from both Loess School of Painting and Chang'an School of Painting, and the flowering movies, television programs, dramas and operas - all these have brought about a a strong "Northwest Wind" all over China.

柳青雕像 ▶
Statue of Liu Qing

丰厚的历史文化积淀孕育了西安的文化艺术，西安撑起了中国文学界的一片天空。陕西当代文学家用自己的热情和真诚为人民抒写，"文学陕军"是陕西当代文学家队伍及中国文坛的一支生力军，尤其在小说方面频频出现脍炙人口的力作。分别写就《创业史》《保卫延安》《平凡的世界》《白鹿原》《浮躁》《青木川》《最后一个匈奴》的柳青、杜鹏程、路遥、陈忠实、贾平凹、叶广芩、高建群……用如椽的大笔记录描写这个时代。陕西这支当代文学家队伍夯实了西安"中国文学重镇"的重要地位，引领了文学创作风潮，是中国文学史上的一道靓丽风景线。

Rich historical and cultural accumulation has given birth to Xi'an culture and art, and Xi'an has propped up a patch of sky in Chinese literature. Shaanxi contemporary writers express their enthusiasm and sincerity for the people. "Shaanxi Writiers Group" is a new force in Shaanxi contemporary writers and Chinese literary society, especially in novel writing. Liu Qing, Du Pengcheng, Lu Yao, Chen Zhongshi, Jia Pingwa, Ye Guangqin and Gao Jianqun, who write such novels as *Builders of a New Life, Defending Yan'an, The Ordinary World, White Deer Plain, Ruined City, Greenwood Riverside and The Last Huns respectively*, recording and describing this era in their masterly ways. This team of contemporary writers has consolidated the important position of Xi'an as "an important city of Chinese literature" by leading the trend of literary creation, which makes up a beautiful landscape in the history of Chinese literature.

人生的道路虽然漫长，但紧要处常常只有几步，特别是当人年青的时候。——柳青

①	②	③
④	⑤	

①当代著名小说家柳青作品——《创业史》
Builders of a New Life by Liu Qing, a famous contemporary novelist

②第三届茅盾文学奖获奖作品路遥——《平凡的世界》
Ordinary World by Lu Yao, winner of Mao Dun Literature Award

③第四届茅盾文学奖获奖作品陈忠实——《白鹿原》
White Deer Plain by Chen Zhongshi, winner of Mao Dun Literature Award

④第十届茅盾文学奖获奖作品陈彦——《主角》
The Protagonist by Chen Yan, winner of the 10th Maodun Literature Award

⑤第八届美孚飞马文学奖铜奖作品贾平凹——《浮躁》
Impetuousness by Jia Pingwa, winner of bronze medal of the 8th Mobil Pegasus Literature Award

西安当代绘画艺术最具代表性的要数长安画派和黄土画派。

以赵望云、石鲁、何海霞、方济众为代表的长安画派，"一手伸向传统，一手伸向生活"，将时代精神与民族传统有机融合，开辟了中国画创作的新路径。继长安画派之后，以刘文西为代表的黄土画派跟进崛起，成为中国画坛一株光彩夺目的奇葩。他们创作的以表现黄土高原古朴倔强为特征的山水画和表现勤劳淳朴的陕北农民形象的人物画，在中国画坛引起轰动。

The most representative of painting art in Xi'an are Chang'an School of Painting and Loess School of Painting.

Chang'an School of Painting, represented by Zhao Wangyun, Shi Lu, He Haixia and Fang Jizhong, "extends one hand to tradition and the other to life", which organically integrates the spirit of the times with national tradition and opens up a new path for Chinese painting creation. After Chang'an School of Painting, the Loess School of Painting represented by Liu Wenxi follows up and becomes a brilliant wonder in Chinese painting world. Their landscape paintings, which are characterized by simplicity and stubbornness of the Loess Plateau, and their figure paintings, which show the industrious and simple image of farmers in northern Shaanxi, have caused a sensation in Chinese painting circles.

◀ 王西京《石鲁》
Wang Xijing's "Shi Lu"

黄土画派由原西安美术学院院长、教授刘文西所创。黄土画派是扎根于黄土地、崛起于黄土地、辉煌于黄土地的美术流派，是以西安美院为主体的学院式画派。该画派画家们的作品风格阳刚豪放、雄浑大气、蓬勃向上，在中国当代现实主义风格绘画中占有重要地位。

Loess School of Painting was founded by Liu Wenxi, former president and professor of Xi'an Academy of Fine Arts. Loess School of Painting is an art school rooted in, growing up and prospering on the yellow land, and it is an academic painting school with Xi'an Academy of Fine Arts as the main body. The style of the painters of this school is masculine and bold, vigorous and powerful, which occupies an important position in Chinese contemporary realistic style painting.

刘文西《沸腾》 ●
Liu Wenxi's "Boiling"

赵望云《事农图》 ▼
Zhao Wangyun's "Farming"

西安影视

Xi'an Film and Television

　　西安的电影和电影人从 1958 年西安电影制片厂成立便满载盛誉，在全国第一个斩获国际 A 级电影节最高奖项，获得国际奖项数量位居全国第一，影片出口量全国第一。从《没有航标的河流》到《老井》《红高粱》，从《西安事变》到《大话西游》，这里先后走出了张艺谋、陈凯歌、王全安、吴天明、顾长卫、黄建新、丁黑等几代著名的电影人和电视人。他们的影视作品《黄土地》《老井》《红高粱》《霸王别姬》《在那遥远的地方》《步入辉煌》《一棵树》《毕业生》《我的 1919》《美丽的大脚》《百鸟朝凤》等，成为中国影史上的经典之作。其中，《老井》《红高粱》成为断代中国电影史的重要力作。

▼ 《那年花开月正圆》获第 31 届中国电视剧飞天奖优秀电视剧奖
"Flowers bloom and the moon is full that year" won the excellent TV Drama Award of The 31th Flying Apsaras Awards

Xi'an films and filmmakers have enjoyed great reputation since the establishment of Xi'an Film Studio in 1958. The studio is the first one in China to win the highest award in the international A-level film festival, ranking first in the number of international awards and the number of film exports in China. From "*The River without a Navigation Mark*" to "*Old Well*" and "*Red Sorghum*", from "*Xi'an Incident*" to "*A Westward Journey*", there have been several generations of famous filmmakers and TV presenters coming out of Xi'an, such as Zhang Yimou, Chen Kaige, Wang Quanan, Wu Tianming, Gu Changwei, Huang Jianxin and Ding Hei. Many of their films and television works, such as "*Yellow Land*", "*Old Well*", "*Red Sorghum*", "*Farewell to My Concubine*", "*In that Distant Place*", "*Stepping into Glory*", "*A Tree*", "*Graduates*", "*My 1919*", "*Beautiful Bigfoot*", "*Hundred Birds and Phoenix*", etc., have become classics in Chinese film history. Among them, "*Old Well*" and "*Red Sorghum*" are the important masterpieces that mark a whole generation in the history of Chinese movies.

咱这地界叫十八里坡，就叫它十八里红吧。

——《红高粱》电影台词

电视剧方面，《大秦帝国》在中央电视台热播。《白鹿原》《那年花开月正圆》分别荣膺国家飞天奖、金鹰奖。2020 年 11 月，根据茅盾文学奖获得者、陕西籍作家陈彦同名小说改编的电视剧《装台》在中央电视台一套播出。

As for TV plays, *"Great Qin Empire"* was a real hit when broadcasted on CCTV. *"White Deer Plain"* and *"Nothing Good Can Stay"* won the National Flying Apsaras Award and Golden Eagle Award. In November 2020, the TV series *"Stage Shifters"*, which was adapted from the novel of the same name by Chen Yan, a Shaanxi writer who won Mao Dun Literature Award, was broadcast on CCTV.

①第 38 届柏林国际电影节金熊奖获奖作品《红高粱》
Red Sorghum, winner of the Golden Bear Award at the 38th Berlin International Film Festival

②根据茅盾文学奖获得者陈彦小说《装台》改编的电视剧——《装台》，在央视播出
The TV series Stage Shifters, which was adapted from the novel of the same name by Chen Yan, the winner of Mao Dun Literature Award, was broadcast on CCTV.

③《建党伟业》
The Founding of a Party

④《大秦赋》
Great Qin Dynasty

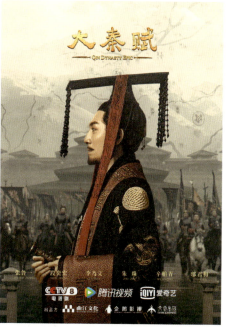

秦腔 Shaanxi Opera

　　秦腔被誉为"中国戏曲鼻祖"，影响和孕育了包括京剧在内的众多剧种，盛于乾隆时期，曲牌丰富，剧目众多，现已发现的秦腔传统剧目有 3000 多种，其唱腔慷慨激越与缠绵悱恻兼具。2006 年被列入第一批国家级非物质文化遗产名录。

　　秦腔艺术代表人物有魏长生、陈雨农、刘毓中等，著名的秦腔科班易俗社，与莫斯科大剧院、英国皇家剧院并称为世界艺坛三大古老剧社。另外，现代秦腔剧《蔡伦》《西京故事》等获得中共中央宣传部组织的精神文明建设"五个一工程"大奖。

Shaanxi Opera, or Qin Opera, the originator of Chinese operas, has influenced and bred many other operas, including Peking Opera. It flourished in Qianlong Period of Qing Dynasty, with rich tunes and numerous repertoires. More than 3,000 traditional repertoires of Qin Opera have been discovered so far, and its singing could be either loud and intense or tender and romantic. In 2006, it was listed on the first batch of national intangible cultural heritages.

The representatives of Shaanxi Opera players are Wei Changsheng, Chen Yunong, Liu Yuzhong, etc. The famous Yisu Art Troupe, together with the Bolshoi Theatre of Russia and the Royal Theatre of the UK, are collectively called the three ancient troupes in the world. In addition, modern Shaanxi operas "*Cai Lun*" and "*Xijing Story*" won the "Five-One Project" Award for Ethic Civilization Construction organized by the Publicity Department of the CPC Central Committee.

鲁迅先生为易俗社题写的『古调独弹』

"The Old Tune Played Anew" for Yisu Opera Club inscribed by Lu Xun

秦腔经典剧目——《三滴血》

Three Drops of Blood, a classic play of Shanxi Opera

2020 年，西安成功举办第 8 届西安国际戏剧节。2021 年 5 月 15—19 日，中国秦腔优秀剧目会演在西安开幕。开幕式演出于 5 月 15 日晚在西安城墙永宁门瓮城举行，演出汇集了 20 多位中国戏剧梅花奖名角。

● 展现百年易俗社发展历程的大型秦腔现代戏——《易俗社》作为唯一一部秦腔剧目亮相第 19 届中国上海国际艺术节
Yisu Art Troupe, a large-scale modern Shaanxi Opera play showing the development of Yisu Art Troupe in the past century, was staged as the only Shaanxi opera program at the 19th Shanghai International Art Festival, China.

In 2020, Xi'an successfully hosted the 8th Xi'an International Drama Festival. On May 15-19, 2021, the performance of outstanding Chinese opera plays was also held in Xi'an. The opening performance was staged in the barbican of Yongning Gate, Xi'an City Wall, on the evening of May 15th. The performance brought together more than 20 famous Chinese Drama Plum Blossom Prize winners.

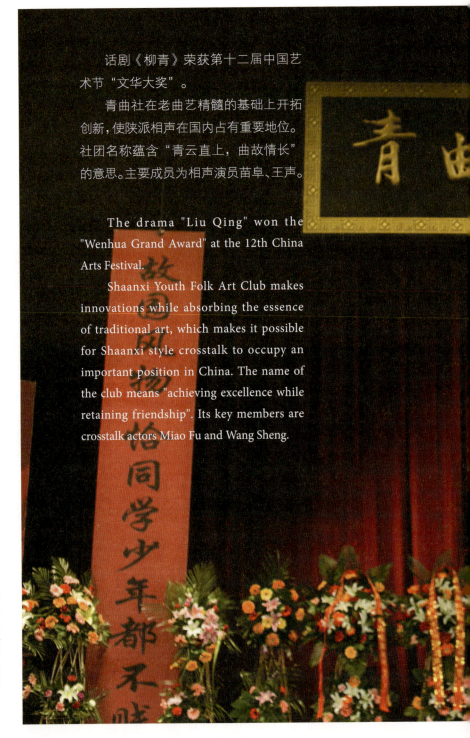

话剧《柳青》荣获第十二届中国艺术节"文华大奖"。

青曲社在老曲艺精髓的基础上开拓创新，使陕派相声在国内占有重要地位。社团名称蕴含"青云直上，曲故情长"的意思。主要成员为相声演员苗阜、王声。

The drama "Liu Qing" won the "Wenhua Grand Award" at the 12th China Arts Festival.

Shaanxi Youth Folk Art Club makes innovations while absorbing the essence of traditional art, which makes it possible for Shaanxi style crosstalk to occupy an important position in China. The name of the club means "achieving excellence while retaining friendship". Its key members are crosstalk actors Miao Fu and Wang Sheng.

青曲社相声表演
Crosstalk performance of Shaanxi Youth Folk Club

《麻醉师》获全国精神文明建设"五个一工程"奖、政府文华奖。

The stage play "Anesthesiologist" is the winner of the "Five-One Project" Award for the National Ethic Civilization Construction and the government's Wenhua Grand Award.

《麻醉师》剧照
The Photograph of Anesthesiologist

文旅融合看今朝
Dynamic Integration of Culture and Tourism

历史与现代、传统与时尚交相辉映，"文化西安"品牌影响力不断扩大。西安文旅融合品牌效应日益凸显，临潼区成为国家首批全域旅游示范区，大唐不夜城入选全国首批高品位步行街试点。《长恨歌》《梦长安——大唐迎宾盛礼》《驼铃传奇》等主题演艺广受好评，曲江"不倒翁"燃爆全网，"打卡西安"成为旅游热点，2020年全年接待海内外游客总数突破3亿人次，旅游业总收入3146亿元，分别增长21.7%和23.1%，获评全球20个热门旅游目的地和全国夜间经济十强城市。2021年5月10日，第五个中国品牌日，人民网研究院联合百度发布的《2021国潮骄傲搜索大数据》显示西安位列"十大热门国潮特色城市"第2名。

大唐芙蓉园彩霞亭 ⬥
Caixia Pavilion in Tang Paradise

History and modernity or tradition and fashion complement each other, and the brand influence of "Cultural Xi'an" expands constantly. The brand effect of Xi'an culture and tourism integration has become increasingly prominent. Lintong District is on the first batch of global tourism demonstration zones in China, and Grand Tang Dynasty Everbright City has been selected as one of the first batch of high-grade pedestrian street pilots in China. Theme performances such as "Song of Everlasting Sorrow", "Dream of Chang'an: Grand Welcome Rite of Tang Dynasty" and "Legend of Camel Bell" are widely received by the public. The "tumbler" in Qujiang has become a hit on the whole network, and "taking snaps at Xi'an" has become a tourist hotspot. The total number of tourists from home and abroad has exceeded 300 million, and the total tourism revenue is 314.6 billion yuan, up by 21.7% and 23.1% respectively. Xi'an has been rated as one of the 20 most popular tourist destinations in the world and one of the top ten cities in the national night-time economy. On May 10, 2021, the fifth China Brand Day, the "2021 National Tide Pride Search Big Data" released by People's Network Research Institute and Baidu showed that Xi'an ranked second among the "Top Ten Popular National Tide Characteristic Cities".

大唐不夜城步行街位于西安市雁塔区的大雁塔脚下，北起大雁塔南广场，南至唐城墙遗址，东起慈恩东路，西至慈恩西路。它也是电视连续剧《长安十二时辰》里长安舆图中晋昌坊和通济坊所在地。丰厚的文化遗产决定了大唐不夜城承担了展示、传播西安城市精神和文化意象的使命。丰富的文化活动和精彩的表演是大唐不夜城成为"网红"景点的特色之一。其中，"不倒翁"的表演在抖音短视频平台成就了 6000 余条表演视频、总播放量超过 15 亿次的奇迹。 2020 年 7 月，大唐不夜城步行街入选首批全国示范步行街名单。

Grand Tang Dynasty Everbright City Located at the foot of Dayan Pagoda in Yanta District, Xi'an City, Shaanxi Province, Grand Tang Dynasty Everbright City extends from South Square of Dayan Pagoda in the north to Tang City Wall Site in the south, and from Ci'en East Road to Ci'en West Road. It is also the location of Jinchang and Tongji quarters in Chang'an Map in Twelve Two-hour Periods of Chang'an. Rich cultural heritage determines its role in undertaking the mission of displaying and spreading the spirit and cultural image of Xi'an City. Rich cultural activities and wonderful performances are one of the characteristics that turn this grand Tang city into an "online celebrity" scenic spot. Among them, the performance of "The Tumbler" has achieved a miracle of more than 6,000 performance videos with a total broadcast volume exceeding 1.5 billion times on the short video platform of Tik Tok. In July 2020, Grand Tang Dynasty Everbright City Pedestrian Street was selected into the list of the first batch of national demonstration pedestrian streets.

大唐不夜城不倒翁表演 ●
The tumbler's performance at Tang
Dynasty Everbright City

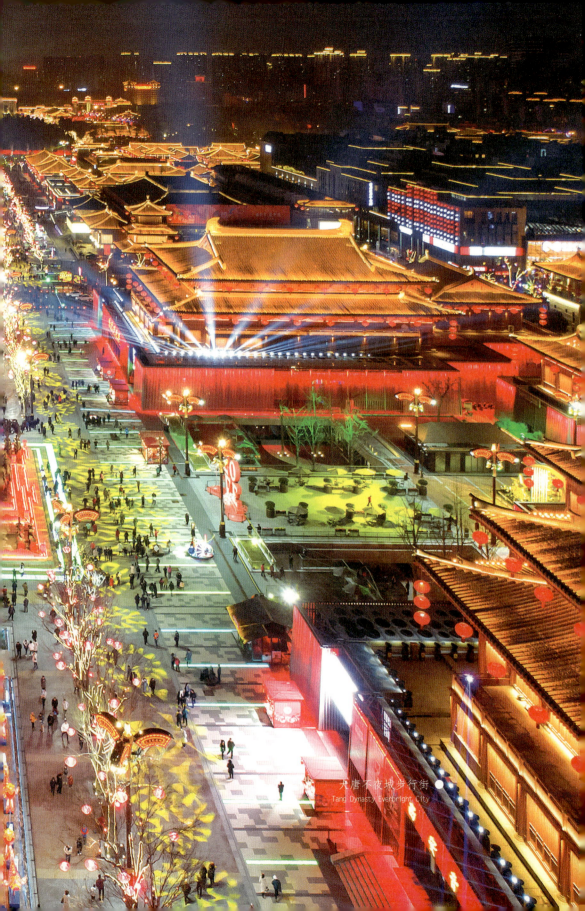

大唐不夜城步行街
Tang Dynasty Everbright City

大唐芙蓉园位于陕西省西安市城南的曲江新区，大雁塔东南侧。它是在原唐代芙蓉园遗址以北，仿照唐代皇家园林式样重新建造的，是中国第一个全方位展示盛唐风貌的大型皇家园林式文化主题公园。

贞观之治后至高宗、睿宗等朝，园林建设开始有了较大的举动，奠定了盛唐文化繁荣的基础。唐玄宗对曲江进行了大规模扩建，使其盛况空前绝后，达到了其园林建设的顶点。经过唐玄宗的扩建，芙蓉园内宫殿连绵，楼亭起伏，曲江的园林建筑达到最高境界，各类文化活动也趋于高潮。

当代大唐芙蓉园在中国乃至世界历史上创造了许多纪录：拥有世界上最大的水幕电影表演、世界上第一个"五感"主题公园、世界上最大的户外香化工程等，还是我国最大的仿唐建筑群。2018 大唐芙蓉园入围"神奇西北 100 景"榜单。

江头宫殿锁千门，细柳新蒲为谁绿？

——【唐】杜甫《哀江头》（节选）

Tang Paradise is located in Qujiang Development Zone, south of Xi'an City, Shaanxi Province, southeast of Big Wild Goose Pagoda. It is rebuilt on the north of the original Furong (lotus) Garden site in Tang Dynasty by following the style of imperial gardens of Tang. It is the first large-scale imperial garden-style cultural theme park in China that displays the style of the prosperous Tang Dynasty in an all-round manner.

From Prosperity of Zhenguan to Emperors Gaozong and Ruizong, the garden construction began to undergo greater changes, which laid the foundation for the prosperity of Tang culture. Emperor Xuanzong expanded Qujiang on a large scale, which made it so unprecedentedly grand that it reached the peak of its garden construction. After the expansion by TangEmperor Xuanzong, in Furong Garden the palaces are continuous and the pavilions undulating. The landscape architecture in Qujiang then reached its highest level, and various cultural activities came to a climax.

The contemporary Tang Paradise has set many records in the history of China and even the world: it has the world's largest waterscape performance, the world's first "five senses" theme park, the world's largest outdoor aromatization project, etc. It is also the largest architectural complex in imitation of Tang Dynasty in China. In 2018, Tang Paradise was put on the list of "100 Magical Northwest Sceneries".

主题演艺

Theme-based Performance

　　主题演艺是推动文化旅游融合的重要实践和艺术载体，从1980年首创推出的中国第一台唐代宫廷乐舞迄今，依托历史文化优势，聚焦特定主题而打造的系列文化演艺活动，成为西安拓展旅游时空、丰富文旅内涵、树立文化自信的重要手段。《仿唐乐舞》是中国最早创作、定型的主题文化旅游演出品牌，打造了驻场常态化演出的标准模式。一票难求的《长恨歌》是中国实景演出国家标准的制定者。以西安事变为主题的大型实景影画《12·12》在全国首创"影画"节目表现形式，是陕西旅游集团华清宫景区继舞剧《长恨歌》后的又一演艺力作，牵手《秦汉风云》《西安千古情》《丝路传奇》《秦豫情》……共同打造"中国演艺之都"。

　　《梦长安——大唐迎宾盛礼》是世界唯一的以盛唐礼仪文化为主题的旅游文化演出，是中国仅有的国宾级迎宾仪式，以行进体验式的表演形式，堪称"天下第一礼"。1996年在世界古都大会首次正式亮相，自2014年提升演变为城墙品牌文化演出，接待过外国元首及贵宾，享誉海内外。

▼ "中华仿古迎宾第一式"——《梦长安——大唐迎宾盛礼》
"The First Scene of Chinese Antique Welcome Ceremony" – Dream of Chang'an: Grand Welcome Rite of Tang Dynasty

Theme-based performance is an important practice and artistic carrier to promote the integration of culture and tourism. Since the first Tang Dynasty court music and dance in China was first launched in 1980s, a series of cultural performing activities based on historical and cultural advantages and focusing on specified themes have become an important means to expand time and space of tourism, to enrich the connotation of cultural tourism and to establish cultural confidence. "Imitated Tang Music and Dance" is the earliest created and finalized theme-based cultural tourism performance brand in China, which has created a standard mode of resident performance. "*Song of Everlasting Sorrow*", for which it is hard to get a ticket, is the setter of the national standard for live performances in China. "12 · 12", a large-scale real-life movie based on the theme of Xi'an Incident, is the first "movie and painting" program expression form in China, and still another masterpiece of performing art in Huaqing Palace Scenic Spot of Shaanxi Tourism Group after the dance drama "*Song of Everlasting Sorrow*". These performances, together with "*Storms of Qin and Han Dynasties*", "*Life-long Romance in Xi'an*", "*Silk Road Legend*" and "Borderless Love", are building Xi'an into "China's Performing Art Capital".

"*Dream of Chang'an: Welcome Ceremony of Tang Dynasty*" is the only tourism cultural performance in the world with the theme of etiquette culture in the prosperous Tang Dynasty, and it is the only state-level welcome ceremony in China. It can be called "the first ceremony in the world" in the form of marching experience. In 1996, it made its debut at the World Ancient Capital Conference, and since 2014, it has evolved into a cultural performance of the city wall brand. It has received many foreign heads of state and distinguished guests, and thus enjoys a good reputation both at home and abroad.

中国首部大型实景历史舞剧《长恨歌》 ●
China's first large-scale live-action historical dance drama *Song of Everlasting Sorrow*

桃李不言自芬芳
Prestigious Institutions of Higher Learning

2020 年，西安在国家教育中心城市中排名第四。作为陕西科教资源的核心承载区，中国最早的教育场所、中国"第一所国立大学"、中国最早的地方学校、中国最早的教育制度、中国完善科举制度……无一不在西安孕育、生发。

中华人民共和国成立后，两次重大生产力先后布局西安。在以交大"西迁精神"为代表的时代精神感召下，一大批高等院校、科研院所、军工单位云集千年古都，奠定了今日西安科技强市、创新名城的重要地位。文化与教育相辅相成，成就当今西安城市的另一种独特魅力。

In 2020, Xi'an ranks fourth among the national education center cities. As the core bearing area of science and education resources in Shaanxi, the earliest place for education, the first national university, "the earliest local school", the earliest education system and the perfect imperial examination system in China are all bred and developed in Xi'an.

After the founding of the People's Republic of China, Xi'an was successively distributed with two major productive forces. Inspired by the spirit of the times represented by the "westward migration spirit" of Jiaotong University, a large number of institutions of higher learning, scientific research institutes and military industrial units gathered in the ancient capital of a thousand years, which has established Xi'an as a powerful city of science and technology and an famous city of innovations today. Culture and education complement each other, providing Xi'an with another special charm.

南洋公学校门 ⬡
Gate of Nanyang College

总五百楹，宏模廓度，伟冠一时。

——《京兆府重修府学记》碑文

西安孔庙始建于唐代，它是中国现存最早的中央最高学府国子监（即太学）的一部分，也是现存最早的唐朝天子圣旨敕办的皇家孔庙。当时在尚书省西隅国子监附近。宋代几经搬迁，崇宁二年（1103）虞策将文庙、府学最终迁建于"府城之东南隅"，即西安碑林博物馆现址，使文庙、碑林、府学同在一处。

Xi'an Confucius Temple was first built in Tang Dynasty. It is a part of the Imperial Academy (Taixue), the earliest existing central institution of higher learning in China. It is also the earliest existing royal Confucius Temple run by the imperial edict of the Emperor of Tang Dynasty. At that time, it was next to the imperial academy in the west corner of Shangshu Department (i.e. department of state affairs). After several relocations in Song Dynasty, in the second year of Chongning of Song Dynasty (1103), Yu Ce finally relocated the Confucius Temple and the government-run school to "the southeast corner of the prefectural city", which is the present site of Xi'an Beilin (Forest of Steles) Museum, making the Confucius Temple, Forest of Steles and government-run school located in the same area.

孔庙 ▶
Confucius Temple

西北联合大学，简称"西北联大"或"联大"，为中国抗日战争时期创立的一所综合性大学。1937年抗日战争爆发后，平津被日军占领，北平大学、国立北平师范大学、国立北洋工学院三所院校于9月10日迁至西安，组成西安临时大学。太原失陷以后，西安临时大学又迁往陕南，不久改名为国立西北联合大学。

这中间发生了许多小故事，其中，著名红学家吴世昌在1938年5月，西北联大发掘丝路开凿者张骞墓及墓前石刻后，撰写了极具民族情怀的《增修汉博望侯张公骞墓碑记》，对张骞"跋涉万里的凿空之功"极尽褒扬，对"国黉播迁，西暨汉中""御侮图强"尽书悲壮，成为西北联大这所战时流亡大学最重要的遗存文献之一。

西北联合大学在抗日战争中形成，在一年多时间里迁校两次，辗转数千里，师生流离跋涉，极为艰苦。其形成和发展，对陕西和西北地区的高等教育事业做出了积极贡献。西北联大在延续和发展中国高等教育上，发挥了承前启后的重要作用；在开发西北和巩固抗战后方上，发挥了拯危救困的重要作用。

Northwest Associated University, referred to as "Associated University" for short, is a comprehensive university founded during the War of Resistance against Japanese Aggression in China. After the outbreak of the War of Resistance against Japan in 1937, Beiping (today's Beijing) and Tianjin were occupied by Japanese troops. Beiping University, National Beiping Normal University and National Beiyang Institute of Technology moved to Xi'an on September 10 to form Xi'an Temporary University. After the fall of Taiyuan City, Xi'an Temporary University moved to southern Shaanxi and soon changed its name to National Northwest Associated University.

Many stories happened during this period. One story goes like this: Wu Shichang, a famous scholar on A Dream of the Red Mansions, wrote in May 1938 "Notes on Repairing the Tombstone of Marquis Zhang Qian" with strong national sentiment after excavating the tomb of Zhang Qian, a Silk Road pioneer in the Han Dynasty. He highly praised Zhang Qian's "accomplishment in travelling thousands of miles to explore new land" and described the sad but stirring feelings of "moving west to Hanzhong" and "working energetically to resist the foreign invasion", which becomes one of the most important existing documents of this exiled university during the war.

Northwest Associated University was formed in the War of Resistance against Japanese Aggression. It was forced to move twice in over a year's time, and traveled thousands of miles. It was extremely difficult for teachers and students to trudge over long distances. Its formation and development made positive contributions to higher education in Shaanxi and Northwest China. This University served as a link between past and future in continuing and developing China's higher education. In addition, it played an important role in developing northwest China and consolidating the rear areas during the war.

国立西北联合大学教职工合影 ◗
Group photo of faculty and staff of
National Northwest Associated University

西安交通大学是上海交通大学以"向科学进军、建设大西北"为集结号，乘坐"交大支援大西北专列"由上海迁往西安，开启了扎根黄土地的创业历程，熔铸了"胸怀大局、无私奉献、弘扬传统、艰苦创业"的西迁精神。

西迁过程中涌现了无数感人肺腑的故事。热工先驱陈大燮作为迁校带头人之一，舍弃了大上海的优越生活环境，卖掉了在上海的房产，义无反顾偕夫人，首批赴西安参加建校工作。1957年，在西安部分新生入学典礼上，陈大燮说："我是交通大学包括上海部分和西安部分的教务长，但我首先要为西安部分的学生上好课。"一席话，坚定了大家献身大西北的决心。

现在的西安交通大学是我国最早兴办、享誉海内外的著名高等学府之一，被国家确定为以建设世界知名高水平大学为目标的教育部直属全国重点大学。2017年入选国家"世界一流大学和一流学科"（简称"双一流"）建设名单A类建设高校。

▼ 西安交通大学南门
South Gate of Xi'an Jiaotong University

Xi'an Jiaotong University came into being because Shanghai Jiaotong University migrated on a "special train of Jiaotong University helping the vast northwest" from Shanghai to Xi'an by answering the call to "march towards science and build Northwest China", which started the entrepreneurial process of taking root in the loessland, and thus forged the westward migration spirit of "bearing in mind the overall situation, making selfless contributions, carrying forward the glorious tradition, and building an enterprise through arduous efforts".

Numerous touching stories happened in the process of moving westward. As one of the leaders for the migration work, Chen Daxie, a pioneer in thermal engineering, abandoned the superior living environment by selling his real estate in Shanghai. He went without hesitation to Xi'an to participate in the construction work with his wife. In 1957, at the entrance ceremony of some freshmen in Xi'an, Chen Daxie said, "I am the provost of Jiaotong University both in Shanghai and in Xi'an, but I must first of all give a good lesson to the students in Xi'an." These words strengthened everyone's determination to dedicating their lives to the northwest.

Today's Xi'an Jiaotong University is one of the earliest world-famous institutions of higher learning in China. It has been identified as a national key university directly under the Ministry of Education with the goal of building a world-famous high-level university. In 2017, it was selected as a Class A Construction Project university in the national list of "first-class universities and first-class disciplines in the world" (referred to as "double first-class").

交大西迁博物馆

Jiaotong University Westward Migration Museum

　　西安是全国重要的科研和高等教育基地，现有各类高校 84 所，其中"双一流"大学中，除上文讲到的西安交通大学，还有西北工业大学、西安电子科技大学、西北农林科技大学。另外，长安大学、陕西师范大学、西北大学等重点高校彰显西安教育实力。

　　西安两院院士 71 人，拥有量位居全国前五。西安还拥有各类科研机构 460 多个，纳入科技统计的科研机构 60 多所。省部级以上重点实验室、工程技术研究中心 340 家。各类专业技术人员近 100 万人，在校学生超百万，每年毕业大学生超过 35 万人。

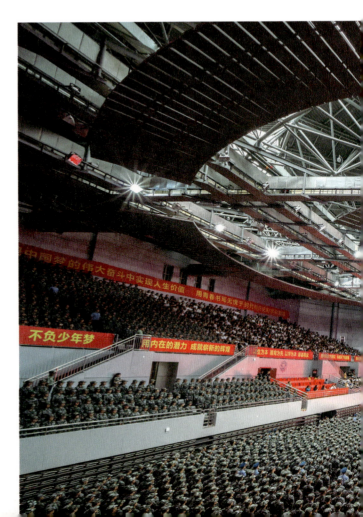

西安电子科技大学开学典礼
Opening Ceremony of Xidian University

Xi'an is an important research and higher education base in China, with 84 universities of various types, among which, besides Xi'an Jiaotong University mentioned above, Northwestern Polytechnical University, Xidian University and Northwest A & F University are "double first-class" universities. In addition, key universities such as Chang'an University, Shaanxi Normal University and Northwest University all manifest the educational strength of Xi'an.

There are 71 academicians in Xi'an, ranking among the top five in China. Xi'an also has more than 460 scientific research institutions of various types, and more than 60 scientific research institutions brought into line with the science and technology statistics. There are 340 key laboratories and engineering technology research centers at or above the provincial level. There are nearly 1 million professional and technical personnel, over one million students at colleges or universities, and more than 350,000 graduates each year.

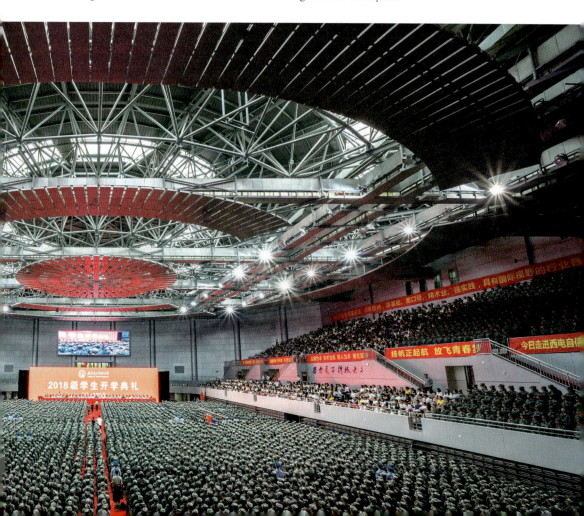

丝路起点 西部引擎

西安

卷四

CHAPTER FOUR STARTING POINT OF SILK ROAD
AND ENGINE FOR THE WESTERN REGIONS

 2020 年中欧班列（西安）
the China-Europe Train "Chang'an"2020

西汉时期，张骞自长安出发凿空西域，伟大的丝绸之路就此开启。千百年来，无数人东来西去，把全球智慧接引回西安，将中国力量远播至地中海和东北亚地区。长安也成为丝绸之路上的商业重镇。斗转星移，初心不改，在国家中心城市、国际化大都市建设目标导引下，西安坚持东西双向互济，陆海两端统筹，打造西部地区对外交往中心、丝路文化高地、内陆开放高地，积极融入以国内大循环为主体、国内国际双循环相互促进的新发展格局，深度融入"一带一路"大格局。

西安港
Xi'an Port

During Western Han Dynasty, Zhang Qian set out from Chang'an to explore the Western Regions, which marks the beginning of the great Silk Road. For thousands of years, global wisdom has been brought back to China while Chinese culture has been disseminated to Xi'an. Chang'an has also become a commercial center on the Silk Road. Under the guidance of the goal of building a national central city and an international metropolis, Xi'an adheres to the principle of two-way mutual aid between east and west, and makes overall plans at both ends of land and sea, so as to build a foreign exchange center, a Silk Road cultural upland and an inland opening upland in the western regions, to actively integrate itself into the new development pattern with domestic circulation as the mainstay and domestic and international double circulation promoting each other, and to move deeper into the "belt and road initiative" frmaework.

凿空之旅起西京
Pathfinders to the Western Regions

闻道寻源使，从天此路回。牵牛去几许，宛马至今来。

——【唐】杜甫《秦州杂诗二十首（其八）》（节选）

丝绸之路起源于西汉，西安是丝绸之路的起点。汉武帝派张骞出使西域，开辟了以首都长安（今西安）为起点，经甘肃、新疆，到中亚、西亚，并连接地中海各国的陆上通道，让东方世界与西方世界开始紧密相连。

张骞（约前164—前114），汉中城固（今陕西城固）人。公元前139年，张骞出使西域，历尽艰险，突破匈奴重围，凿空联通东西的丝绸之路，自此"无数铃声遥过碛，应驮白练到安西"，为欧亚大陆整体性文明与进步注入了强大的东方智慧。

Silk Road originated in Western Han Dynasty, and Xi'an was its starting point. Emperor Wudi of Han Dynasty sent Zhang Qian on a mission to the Western Regions, opening up a land passage from the capital Chang'an (now Xi'an) to Central Asia and West Asia through Gansu and Xinjiang, and finally to the Mediterranean countries, so the east and the west began to be closely connected.

Zhang Qian (? —114 B.C.), a native of Chenggu, Hanzhong (today's Chenggu, Shaanxi). In 139 B.C., Zhang Qian went on a diplomatic journey to the Western Regions. He went through all kinds of hardships, broke through layer upon layer of encirclement of Huns, and finally opened Silk Road connecting the east and the west. From then on, "countless camels moved at their best, carrying white silk to the west". By this means, powerful oriental wisdom has been instilled into the overall civilization and progress of Eurasia.

大唐丝路盛景图（局部）　雒建安画
Grand View of Silk Road in Tang Dynasty (part) painting by Luo Jian'an

班超（32—102），字仲升，扶风郡平陵县（今陕西咸阳）人。永平十六年（73），班超投笔投戎，跟随大将军窦固征讨匈奴，镇压安抚西域各国。经过31年的努力，西域与汉断绝65年的关系终于恢复。班超平定了西域50多个国家，为恢复东汉对西域的统治、巩固我国西部疆域、促进多民族国家发展做出了卓越的贡献。同时，也为保卫丝绸之路，促进中国和中亚、西亚各国的经济文化交流做出了巨大贡献。

Ban Chao (32-102), also called Zhongsheng, was a native of Pingling County, Fufeng Prefecture (now Xianyang, Shaanxi Province). In the 16th year of Yongping Period (73), Ban Chao gave up his civilian pursuits to join the army, and then followed General Dou Gu to fight the huns and to suppress and appease the western countries. Through 31 years' efforts, the relationship between the Western Regions and Han, which had been cut off for 65 years, finally recovered. Ban Chao pacified more than 50 countries in the Western Regions, and made outstanding contributions to restoring Eastern Han Dynasty's rule there, consolidating China's western territory and promoting the development of a multi-ethnic country. At the same time, he also made great contributions to defending the Silk Road and promoting economic and cultural exchanges between China and those countries in Central Asia and West Asia.

货殖天下一时雄
Trade Center in the World

　　到唐代时，"丝路贸易"达到顶峰，唐都长安是当时世界上最大的国际城市之一。驼队将中国大批的珠宝、丝绸、瓷器等从长安城开远门运往西域各国及地区，而西域的外国商人也通过丝绸之路将香料、药物等运到长安，这些货物主要集结于长安外郭城西城区和设店于开远门内附近的国际贸易市场——西市。据《唐六典》记载，唐廷对外国人在中国的活动及移居持较为宽容的态度，以致迁居大唐的外国人士往往数以万计。在东、西两市及其周边诸坊，形成了规模较大的外国人聚集圈。东市与西市逐渐成为丝绸之路上最繁华的贸易中心。

By Tang Dynasty, "Silk Road Trade" reached its peak, and Chang'an, capital of Tang Dynasty, was one of the largest international cities in the world at that time. From Chang'an City, a huge amount of Chinese jewellery, silk, porcelain and so on was transported to western countries and regions by camel teams. The so-called "Hu merchants" from the Western Regions also transported spices and medicines to Chang'an through the Silk Road. They mainly gathered in West District of outer city of Chang'an, and opened stores in the West Market, an international trade market in the neighboring area inside Kaiyuan Gate. According to the records of Six Codes of Tang Dynasty, the Tang court took a more tolerant attitude towards the activities and emigration of Hu people (from the Western Regions) in China, so that tens of thousands of Hu people often moved to settle down in Tang Dynasty. In the east and west markets and their surrounding quarters, large-scale communities of Hu people emerged. East and west markets gradually became two of the most prosperous trade centers on the Silk Road.

丝路起点重现辉煌——大唐西市 ▼
Tang West Market – reemerging prosperity at the starting point of Silk Road

东市 East Market

旋见衣冠就东市，忽遗弓剑不西巡。

——【唐】杜牧《河湟》

东市是唐代长安最大的商业聚集地之一，位于长安城东。街道两侧有铁行、肉行、麸行、金银行、绢行、药行等货财 220 行，经营各种商品的坐商近千家。市内又有很多专供中外客商寄存和出售货物的邸店和饮食摊点、旗亭酒肆、旅舍客馆等。由于京师王公百官的居住宅第多在城东，靠近该市，故这里商贾辐辏，商业贸易异常活跃。

East Market, located in the east of Chang'an, was one of the largest commercial gathering places in Chang'an in Tang Dynasty. On both sides of the street, there were 220 categories of goods, such as iron, meat, bran, gold and silver, silk and medicine, with nearly 1,000 traders of various commodities. In the city, there were also many hotels, food stalls, pubs, hostels and guest houses dedicated to storing and selling goods by Chinese and foreign merchants. Because most of the residences of the nobles and officials in the capital were in the east of the city, close to the market, the merchants here were concentrated and the commerce and trade were extremely active.

西市 *West Market*

西市位于长安城西，是唐代长安主要的工商业区和经济活动中心，又是国际贸易的市场，较东市更为繁荣，而五行中的金，于位为西，故唐人又称西市为"金市"。李白《少年行》诗云："五陵年少金市东，银鞍白马度春风。落花踏尽游何处，笑入胡姬酒肆中。"西市街宽各百步，两侧有称行、大衣行、金银行、鞦辔行等，经营各种商品交易的商贾近千家。大街四周又设有很多邸店、旅舍、旗亭酒肆及饮食摊点。通过丝绸之路来到长安经商的西域商贾也多聚集该市，或开设酒店、旅舍，或经营金银珠宝等买卖。

经游天下遍，却到长安城。
城中东西市，闻客次第迎。
——【唐】元稹《估客乐》（节选）

▼ 今大唐西市一景
A Scene of Tang West Market

大唐西市博物馆 ⬢
Tang West Market Museum

West Market, located in the west of Chang'an, was the main industrial and commercial district and economic activity center of Chang'an in Tang Dynasty. And it was also the market of international trade, more prosperous than East Market. According to Chinese philosophy, the gold in the Five Elements lies in the west, so the Tang people also called West Market "Gold Market". Li Bai's poem "*A Youth's Travel*" says, "A young man lived west of Gold Market, and rode on a silver-saddled horse to enjoy the spring breeze. Having watched all the blossoms in CHang'an, he strolled smiling into a hun's pub. " Each of the streets in West Market was 100 steps wide, with shops selling scales, coats, gold and silver, bridles, etc. on both sides. There were nearly 1,000 merchants engaged in various commodity transactions. Many mansions, hostels, pubs and food stalls could be found along the main street. Most of foreign merchants coming from the Western Regions through the Silk Road often gathered in West Market, opening restaurants and hostels, or engaged in gold, silver and jewelry businesses.

万国衣冠拜冕旒
Frequent International Exchanges

丝绸之路既是商品贸易之路，亦是文明互鉴之路。张骞通使西域后，源始自古印度的佛教沿丝绸之路自西而东，渐次传入中原王朝。鸠摩罗什、玄奘等人有力地促进了文化的双向交流。

公元7世纪初至9世纪末，260余年里日本先后19次向唐朝派出遣唐使团，频度之密、规模之大、时间之久、内容之丰，创造了中日文化交流史上的空前盛举。空海、阿倍仲麻吕（晁衡）、鉴真等人，是这一时期中日友好交流的典型代表。

唐王朝开放繁荣、昌盛自信。大唐一度同300多个国家和地区建立了外交联系，国都长安堪称人类历史上第一座国际化大都市，拥有当时世界上最大的商贸中心——大唐西市。百万市民中外国侨民多达10万人，其中3000多名外国人在唐朝从政，佐证了长安独一无二的国际地位和世界级影响力。

Silk Road is not only a road of merchandise trade, but also a road of mutual learning among civilizations. After Zhang Qian was sent on a diplomatic mission to the Western Regions, Buddhism, which originated from Ancient India, was gradually introduced into China along the Silk Road from west to east, from boder areas to the inland. Kumarajiva, Xuan Zang and others have effectively promoted the two-way cultural exchange.

From the beginning of the 7th century to the end of the 9th century, Japan sent 19 diplomatic delegations to Tang Dynasty in over 260 years. These frequent large-scalee, long-lasting and content-rich visits have created an unprecedented event in the history of Sino-Japanese cultural exchanges. Kong Hai, Abe Zhongmalu (Chao Heng), Jian Zhen and others are typical representatives of Sino-Japanese friendly exchanges during this period.

Tang Dynasty was open, prosperous and confident. It once established diplomatic ties with more than 300 countries and regions. Chang'an, the capital of Tang, was the first international metropolis with a population of over one million in human history, and had the largest business center in the world at that time—Tang West Market. There were as many as 100,000 foreign residents among amillion of citizens, among which more than 3,000 foreigners became government officials of Tang Dynasty, which established Chang'an's unique international status and world-class influence.

彩绘胡人骑驼俑
Colored Nomad on a Camel

东方风来满眼春
New Missions for the Ancient Capital City

　　经历过烟花绽放时的绚烂，也历经了低谷时的悄然，如今的西安带着长安的基因和记忆重回国际都市行列。当前，西安正肩负着打造西部地区对外交往中心、丝路文化高地、内陆开放高地，加快建设国家中心城市、具有历史文化特色的国际化大都市的国家使命和发展重任。

　　2016 年 8 月，党中央、国务院决定在陕西省设立自由贸易试验区，助力西安打造内陆改革开放高地，推动由商品和要素流动型开放向规则等制度型开放转变。2019 年，西安获评"2019 国际物流大通道建设突出贡献城市"，入选首批国家物流枢纽建设名单。作为陕西自贸区核心片区，西安国际港务区依托西安地理空间、交通区位，发挥中国唯一拥有国际、国内双代码内陆港口制度优势，加快推进中欧班列集结中心示范工程建设。2019 年，中欧班列"长安号"全年开行 2133 列，增长 70%，开行量、重载率、货运量稳居全国前列。截至 2020 年，中欧班列"长安号"覆盖 45 个国家和地区开行 3720 列，位居全国第一。2021 年 4 月 1 日起，西安国际港站正式揭牌启用，这标志着西安港深度融入亚欧陆海贸易大通道和全球铁路网络体系。

陕西自由贸易试验区
Shaanxi Pilot Free Trade Zone

Xi'an has experienced the splendor of prosperous times and the silence of low ebb at other times. Now Xi'an has now returned to the ranks of international cities with the genes and memories of Chang'an. At present, Xi'an is shouldering the national mission and development responsibility of building a foreign exchange center, a Silk Road cultural upland and an inland opening upland in the western region, and accelerating the construction of a national central city and an international metropolis with historical and cultural characteristics.

In August 2016, the CPC Central Committee and the State Council decided to set up a free trade pilot zone in Shaanxi Province, supporting Xi'an in becoming a vanguard of reform and opening up in China's inland region, and promoting its transformation from commodity and factor flow opening up model to rules and other institutions opening up model. In 2019, Xi'an was appraised as a city with outstanding contribution to the construction of international logistics channel 2019, and was selected into the list of the first batch of national logistics hub construction. As the core area of Shaanxi Free Trade Zone, Xi'an International Port Area, relying on Xi'an's geographical space and traffic location, takes advantage of China's only international and domestic dual-code inland port system to accelerate the construction of the demonstration project of China-Europe train assembly center. By 2019, the China-Europe Train "Chang'an" had been operated with 2,133 trains in the whole year, an increase of 70%, and its operation volume, heavy load rate and freight volume ranked first in the country. In 2020, the China-Europe Train "Chang'an" operated with a total of 3,720 trains, ranking first in China. From April 1, 2021, Xi'an International Port Station was officially opened, which marks the deep integration of Xi'an Port into the Asia-Europe land-sea trade channel and the global railway network system.

2019 年 11 月，西安作为中国和亚太区唯一代表，成功当选世界城地组织联合主席城市。当选双"联合主席"是新时代西安城市发展成就的世界级确认，是西安国际化大都市建设历程中的重大事件，为西安经济社会实现高质量发展赋予了新的能级。

截至 2020 年，已有泰国、韩国、柬埔寨、马来西亚 4 个国家在西安设立总领事馆。西安可办理法国、荷兰、西班牙等 20 余国别的签证业务，与 37 个城市缔结为国际友好城市，与 36 个国家的 67 个城市缔结为国际友好交流城市，在四大洲 18 个国家设立了 21 个西安海外侨务工作联络点。

◗ 西安港
Xi'an Port

In November 2019, Xi'an, as the only representative of China and the Asia-Pacific regions, was successfully elected as the co-chairman city of the World Cities Organization, which means a world-class confirmation of Xi'an's urban development achievements in the new era and is a major event in the process of Xi'an's international metropolis construction. This endows Xi'an with a new level of energy in achieving high-quality economic and social development.

By 2020, four countries including Thailand, South Korea, Cambodia and Malaysia had established consulates in Xi'an, which could handle visa services for more than 20 countries including France, the Netherlands and Spain. Besides, Xi'an had established closer ties with 37 cities as its sister cities and with 67 cities in 36 countries as international friendly exchange cities, and opned 21 liaison offices for overseas Chinese from Xi'an in 18 countries on four continents.

近年来，西安全方位扩大国际合作交流，成功举办欧亚经济论坛、全球硬科技创新大会、全球创投峰会、中国国际通用航空大会等大型展会活动，承办国际大会及会议协会（ICCA）认定的国际会议数量位列全国第四。丝绸之路国际艺术节、丝绸之路国际电影节、丝绸之路国际旅游博览会等大型人文交流活动陆续在西安举办，"一带一路"海关高层论坛、丝绸之路旅游部长会议、西安国际马拉松等异彩纷呈的国际交流活动让西安这座城青春澎湃、熠熠生辉。2021年5月，第五届丝绸之路国际博览会在西安举办，继续构建国际化合作平台。

In recent years, Xi'an has expanded international cooperation and exchanges in all respects. It has successfully hosted large-scale exhibition activities such as Eurasian Economic Forum, Global Hard Science and Technology Innovation Conference, Global Venture Capital Summit, China International Navigation Conference, etc. The number of international conferences and conferences recognized by ICCA ranks fourth in China. Large-scale cultural exchange activities such as Silk Road International Art Festival, Silk Road International Film Festival and Silk Road Tourism International Expo have been held in Xi'an one after another. The spectacular international exchange activities such as "Belt and Road Initiative" Customs High-level Forum, Silk Road Tourism Ministers Meeting and Xi'an International Marathon have made Xi'an a city full of youth and brilliance. In May, 2021, the 5th Silk Road International Expo was held in Xi'an, and the international cooperation platform continued to be built.

🔺 丝绸之路国际电影节
Silk Road International Film Festival

🔺 西商大会
Xi'an Entrepreneurs Conference

区域发展看西安
A Model for Regional Development

  继往开来，再续新章，西安正以奋力建设国家中心城市为航标，乘风破浪，勇立潮头，迈向"西部地区重要的经济中心"历史方位。西安，古老的文明在各个方面得以传承，辉煌明亮的现代城市画卷中，经济繁荣，产业兴盛是最浓墨重彩的一笔。

  党的十八大以来，同力重工、三星12英寸闪存芯片二期二阶段、法士特年产20万台S变速器智能工厂、比亚迪高端智能终端产业园等重大项目的快速建设，将为西安经济发展增添新动能。

  党的十八大以来，西安咸阳国际机场航线网络通达能力居全国十大机场第二位，国内业务增速居全国十大机场第三位。西安北站有18个站台34股道，是目前亚洲站台股道数最多、站场规模最大的高铁站。2020年12月，银西高铁进入试运行阶段。至此，西安刷新高铁城市"朋友圈"，基本覆盖了全国81%的主要城市。

  党的十八大以来，火车站综合交通枢纽工程、高铁北站立体交通枢纽工程、朱宏路—凤城五路立交、元朔大道—西铜高速立交、地铁14号线、奥体大道跨绕城高速立交、锦堤六路下穿灞河隧道、北辰永淳路隧道等重点项目集中建成通车。

Building on past achievements and striving for new progress, Xi'an is makingng great strides in building a national central city through greater efforts and with more courage. It is now moving ahead towards the historical position of "a key economic center in the western region". In Xi'an, the ancient civilization has been passed down in all aspects, and in the brilliant and bright spectacle of the modern city, economic prosperity and industrial bloom are its preeminent features.

Since 2021, the rapid construction of Tongli Heavy Industry, Samsung 12-inch Flash Chip (Phase II, Stage II), Fast Technology's Intelligent Factory with an annual output of 200,000 S transmissions, BYD High-end Intelligent Terminal Industrial Park and other major projects will add new kinetic energy to Xi'an's economic development.

Xi'an Xianyang International Airport ranks second in terms of airline network accessibility and third regarding domestic business growth by 2018. Xi'an North Railway Station, with 18 platforms and 34 tracks, is one of the largest high-speed railway stations in Asia. In December 2020, Yinchuan-Xi'an high-speed railway began its trial operation. So far, Xi'an has refreshed its "friend circle" of high-speed railway cities, covering 81% of major cities in China.

Since 2021, key projects such as railway station comprehensive transportation hub project, high-speed railway north station three-dimensional transportation hub project, Zhuhong Road-Fengcheng 5 Road interchange, Yuanshuo Avenue-Xitong Expressway interchange, Metro Line 14, Olympic Sports Avenue overpass, Jindi 6 Road through Bahe Tunnel, Beichen Yongchun Road Tunnel and so on have been completed and opened to traffic.

运－20飞机
Y-20 Military Transport Aircraft

西安依托三星、陕汽、西飞、西电、西部超导、杨森等龙头企业，做强电子信息制造、汽车、航空航天、高端装备制造、新材料新能源、生物医药等6大支柱产业；依托华为、中兴、铂力特等龙头企业，做大人工智能、机器人产业、5G产业、增材制造、大数据与云计算产业等5大新兴产业；同步做优现代金融、现代物流、研发设计、检验检测认证、软件和信息服务、会议会展等6大生产性服务业，展现西安独一无二的产业优势和极具竞争力的产业布局。党的十八大以来，吸引了203家世界500强企业落户西安。

2021年上半年，西安市生产总值5099.62亿元，同比增长7.8%；两年平均增长5.3%。其中，第一产业增加值109.05亿元，同比增长3.0%，两年平均增长2.3%；第二产业增加值1654.25亿元，同比增长6.3%，两年平均增长5.9%；第三产业增加值3336.32亿元，同比增长8.8%，两年平均增长5.0%。

Xi'an depends on the leading enterprises such as Samsung, Shaanxi Automobile, Xi'an Aircraft, Western Electric, Western Superconductor and Janssen to strengthen six pillar industries such as electronic information manufacturing, automobile, aerospace, high-end equipment, new materials and new energy, and biomedicine. It also depends on such leading enterprises as Huawei, ZTE and Bright Laser Technologies (BLT) to expand five emerging industries such as artificial intelligence, robotics, 5G technology, additive manufacturing, and big data and cloud computing. At the same time, it is endeavoring to promote the six major productive service industries, including modern finance; modern logistics; research, development and design; inspection, testing and certification; software and information services; and conferences and exhibitions. By 2018, it had attracted 203 Fortune Global 500 enterprises to settle in Xi'an because of its unique advantages in scientific research, industry and location.

In the first half of 2021, the GDP of Xi'an was 509.962 billion yuan, a year-on-year increase of 7.8%, and an average growth of 5.3% in two years. Among them, the added value of the primary industry was 10.905 billion yuan, up 3.0% year on year, with an average increase of 2.3% in two years. The added value of the secondary industry was 165.425 billion yuan, with a year-on-year increase of 6.3% and an average annual growth rate of 5.9% in both years. And the added value of the tertiary industry was 333.632 billion yuan, up 8.8% year on year, with an average increase of 5.0% in two years.

2013 年 6 月 11 日，由位于西安航天产业基地的航天科技集团六院 7103 厂研制生产主动力发动机的神舟十号飞船发射升空。

On June 11th, 2013, Shenzhou-10 spacecraft, which was developed and produced by No. 7103 Factory of the Sixth Academy of Aerospace Science and Technology Group in Xi'an Aerospace Industry Base, was launched into space.

西安以建设与国家中心城市相适应的现代农业为目标，坚持产业为先、融合为媒，着力打造绿色安全、优质高效的都市现代农业，推动农业农村发展再上新台阶，形成了鄠邑区葡萄基地、周至县猕猴桃基地、临潼区石榴基地、阎良区甜瓜基地等特色农业。

　　2020年投入使用的西安丝路国际会议中心是西北地区功能最齐备、面积最大的综合性会议中心，是我国现代化的超大型会展中心之一。

Xi'an takes the construction of modern agriculture suitable for the national central city as its goal. By adhering to the principle of developing industries first and focusing on integration as the medium, it strives to build green, safe, high-quality and efficient urban modern agriculture, and promotes the development of agriculture and rural areas to a new level. In this way, some characteristic agriculture groups such as grape base in Huyi District, kiwifruit base in Zhouzhi County, pomegranate base in Lintong District and melon base in Yanliang District have come into shape.

Xi'an Silk Road International Conference Center, which was put into use in 2020, is a comprehensive conference center with the most complete functions and the largest area in Northwest China, and is one of the modern super-sized exhibition centers in China.

西安高新区中铁西安中心 ▼
China Railway Xi'an Center in Xi'an High-tech Zone

科技创新铸新风
Scientific and Technological Innovation

从"两弹一星"到载人航天，从探月工程到载人深潜，从C919大型客机到"复兴号"动车组列车……中华人民共和国70余年科技史，处处闪耀着"西安科技"的璀璨光华。

"西安航天智造"为中国航天事业做出了重要贡献。在我国北斗三号全球卫星导航系统最后一颗组网卫星的发射任务中，航天五院西安分院承担了该卫星全部有效载荷的研制任务。长征三号乙运载火箭的发动机由航天六院制造。位于西安的771所为该卫星配备了"最强大脑"，在北斗三号系统成功完成全球组网中发挥了重要作用。中航工业西安飞机工业集团制造的运-20成为中国自行研制的第一种大型战略运输机，亚洲人独立自主制造的最大的运输机。2021年6月17日，神舟十二号载人飞船发射升空，位于西安的771研究所、航天六院、航天五院西安分院为本次航天任务的顺利完成贡献了重要力量。

From "two nuclear bombs and one satellite" to manned spaceflight, from lunar exploration project to manned deep diving, from C919 large passenger plane to "Fuxing" EMU train ... "Xi'an Science and Technology" always shines brilliantly in the 70-year history of science and technology in New China.

"Xi'an Aerospace Intelligence" has made important contributions to China's aerospace industry. In the launching mission of the last networking satellite of Beidou-3 global satellite navigation system in China, Xi'an Branch of the Fifth Academy of Aerospace undertook the task of developing all the payloads of the satellite. Long March 3B's engine was manufactured by the Sixth Academy of Aerospace. The No. 771 Institute located in Xi'an equipped the satellite with "super brain", which played an important role in the successful completion of the global networking of Beidou-3 system. Yun-20, manufactured by AVIC Xi'an Aircraft Industry Group, became the first strategic transport aircraft developed by China and the largest transport aircraft independently manufactured by Asians.

位于西安市临潼区的中国科学院国家授时中心："北京时间"西安制造 ●

National Time Service Center of Chinese Academy of Sciences in Lintong District, Xi'an: "Beijing Time" made in Xi'an

西安是全国科研活动最为活跃的城市之一，年均 R&D（科学研究与试验发展）投入达 5.1% 以上，高于全国均值 2.91 个百分点。得益于科研沃土的滋养，孕育出众多优秀科技成果。2018 年，发明专利拥有量 35383 件，每万人发明专利拥有量达 35.4 件，是全国平均水平的 3.07 倍，位列 15 个副省级城市第四位。技术成果交易活跃，年均技术市场交易额 1000 亿元，稳居全国副省级城市之首。2019 年国家科学技术奖三大类中，西安占 19 项，获奖数量位居全国前列。

北斗授时
Beidou Time Service

Xi'an is one of the most active cities in scientific research activities in China, with an average annual research and development investment of over 5.10%, which is 2.91 percent higher than the national average. Thanks to the nourishment of fertile soil for scientific research in Xi'an, many outstanding scientific and technological achievements have been made. In 2018, the number of invention patents was 35,383, and the number of invention patents per 10,000 people reached 35.4, which was 3.07 times the national average and ranked fourth among 15 sub-provincial cities. Transaction of technological achievements is also active, with an average annual turnover of 100 billion yuan in technology market, ranking first among sub-provincial cities in China. Among the three categories of national science and technology awards in 2019, Xi'an won 19 awards, and the number of awards ranked among the top in the country.

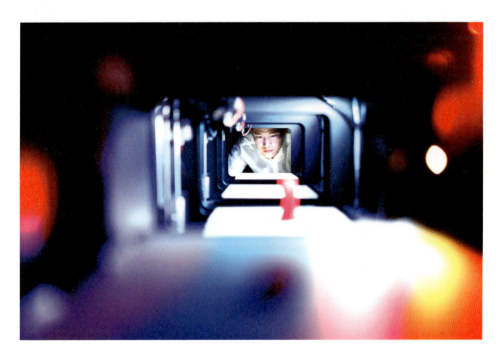

2015 年 4 月 26 日，陕西省工业设计工程实验室，西北工业大学三年级硕士研究生田超在 ⬤ 利用 3D 打印机打印产品样件。3D 打印技术的普及，大大缩短了新产品的研制周期。

On April 26, 2015, Tian Chao, a third-year graduate student of Northwestern Polytechnical University in Shaanxi Industrial Design and Engineering Laboratory, was using a 3D printer to print product samples. The popularity of 3D printing technology has greatly shortened the development cycle of new products.

🔺 2020 年 11 月 24 日，"嫦娥五号"月球探测器发射升空，位于西安的中国航天科技集团六院、五院西安分院、四院、九院 771 所，以及西安卫星测控中心等单位都在这次发射任务中承担了重要职责。

On November 24, 2020, the "Chang'e-5" lunar probe was launched. The Sixth Academy, the Xi'an Branch of the Fifth Academy, the Fourth Academy and No. 771 Institute of the Ninth Academy of China Aerospace Science and Technology Group in Xi'an, and the Xi'an Satellite Measurement and Control Center all assumed important responsibilities in this launch mission.

以"硬科技推动高质量发展"为主题的 2020 全球硬科技创新大会在西安举办 ⬛
The Global Hard Technology Innovation Conference2020 with the theme of "Hard Technology Promoting High Quality Development" was held in Xi'an.

　　近年来，西安以"硬科技"为引领，大力发展硬科技"八路军"，设立硬科技产业基金，布局硬科技尖端项目，孵化培育硬科技企业。2018 年以来，由西安光机所首倡提出的"硬科技"理论进入国家话语体系。西安现有高新技术企业 3673 家，科技型中小企业 4145 家，其中瞪羚企业 200 余家。2019 年 3 家科技企业成功上市科创版，排名西部城市第一，成为世界科技前沿的重要聚焦城市。

In recent years, Xi'an has taken "hard technology" as the guide and vigorously developed another "eighth route army" of hard technology by setting up a hard technology industry fund, laying out cutting-edge projects of hard technology, and hatching and cultivating hard technology enterprises. Since 2018, the "hard science and technology" theory initiated by Xi'an Institute of Optics and Mechanics has entered the national discourse system. There are 3,673 high-tech enterprises and 4,145 small and medium-sized science and technology enterprises in Xi 'an, including more than 200 gazelle enterprises. In 2019, 3 tcchnology companies were successfully listed on the Science and Technology Innovation Board, ranking first among cities in west China and becoming an important focus city in the forefront of world science and technology.

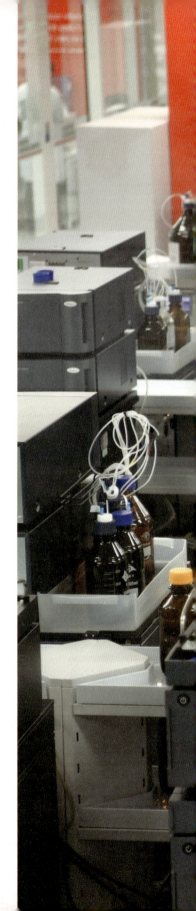

目前，西安正紧抓第三次重大生产力布局机遇，面向国家科技战略和前沿科技发展需求，争创我国第四个、西部第一个综合性国家科学中心，通过培育国际一流的重大科技基础设施集群和研发机构群落，加快高端科技创新资源要素集聚，提升我国在交叉前沿领域的源头创新能力和科技综合实力，形成以西安为龙头，带动西北五省，辐射"一带一路"沿线国家和地区，建设具有国际影响的科技创新中心，开创产业发展和城市建设深度融合的新局面。

At present, Xi'an, by seizing the opportunity of the third major distribution of productive forces and being geared to the national science and technology strategy and to the demand for cutting-edge science and technology development, is striving for the establishment of the fourth comprehensive national science center in China and the first comprehensive national science center in the west. By cultivating world-class major science and technology infrastructure clusters and research and development institutions, Xi'an is accelerating the gathering of high-end scientific and technological innovation resources, and improving China's source innovation ability and comprehensive scientific and technological strength in the cross-cutting frontier areas. This is to build a science and technology innovation center with international influence, with Xi'an as the leader, the five provinces in nortwest China developed and the countries and regions along "Belt and Road" stumulated. In this way, a new phase is to be created in terms of industry development and urban construction deeply integrated.

中国最大的合资制药企业——西安杨森制药有限公司 ▶
Xi'an Janssen Pharmaceutical Co., Ltd., the largest pharmaceutical joint venture in China

幸福宜居新典范
A Happy and Habitable City

2020 年，西安第九次蝉联中国最具幸福感的城市。十三朝古都丰厚的遗产，通过美食、民间技艺、民俗融汇到了当代西安人的日常当中。看似不起眼的一碗泡馍、一段唱腔、一种技艺、一个民俗时节都能追溯出千年之前的味道。

如今的西安商圈繁荣、书卷飘香，绿荫摇曳，幸福满容，展现着这里最年轻、最宜居的风采；如今的西安不断发挥城市优势，扩大对外交流，为共筑人类命运共同体不懈努力。

In 2020, Xi'an was elected the happiest city in China for the ninth time. The rich heritage of the ancient capital of thirteen dynasties has been integrated into the daily life of contemporary Xi'an people through food, folk artistry and folk customs. A seemingly unremarkable bowl of chopped-up baked buns soaked in broth, a piece of Shaanxi opera, an artistry and a folk custom can be traced back to hundreds or even thousands of years ago.

The businesses are flourishing, the books smell fragrant, the trees make a pleasant shade, and there is a happy smile on everyone's face. The youngest and most habitable are the demeanours of Xi'an. Contemporary Xi'an constantly exerts its urban advantages, expands foreign exchanges and makes unremitting efforts to play its own part in building a community of common destiny.

西安菜汇南北、味通东西，是一座名副其实的美食之城。西安的饮食文化开创于周秦，兴盛于盛唐。中国最早的宫廷宴"周八珍"；唐时最豪华的"烧尾宴"，最雅致的"曲江游宴"都在这里。《陕西烹饪大典》记载，从周到唐的古典名菜，就有二百多种。市井小吃，老字号更是不胜枚举，让西安城充满了市井生活气息。

Xi'an cuisine assembles foods from north and south and integrates flavors from east and west, making it a veritable gourmet city. Xi'an food culture originated in Zhou and Qin Dynasties and flourished in the prosperous Tang Dynasty. China's earliest banquet "eight delicacies of Zhou", the most luxurious "burning tail banquet" (to express gratitude or to celebrate promotion) and the most elegant "Qujiang tour banquet" in Tang Dynasty can be found here. Shaanxi Cooking Ceremony records that there are more than 200 kinds of famous classical dishes from Zhou to Tang dynasties. Street snacks and time-honored brand foods, too numerous to mention one by one, fill Xi'an with vitality of life.

回民街
The Hui Min Street

陕西省非物质文化遗产——肉夹馍
Chinese Hamburger — an intangible cultural heritage of Shaanxi Province

陕西十大经典名菜之——葫芦鸡
Gourd chicken, one of the top ten classic dishes in Shaanxi

油饼
Deep-fried Dough Cake

biangbiang 面
Biangbiang Noodles

陕西省非物质文化遗产——水盆羊肉
Water-basin Mutton Broth – an intangible cultural heritage of Shaanxi Province

羊肉泡馍
Chopped-up Baked Buns Soaked in Mutton Broth

从"增绿"工程、"水润"工程入手，西安着力改善市民生活环境。浐灞国家湿地公园、曲江池遗址公园、昆明池遗址公园、长安公园、灞桥生态湿地公园、渭河城市绿地运动公园等一批公园相继建成。城市增绿成效显著，荣获"国家森林城市"称号。

Starting with the "greening" and "water conservancy" projects, Xi'an has made great efforts to improve the living environment of its citizens. A number of parks such as Chanba National Wetland Park, Qujiang Pond Ruins Park, Kunming Pond Ruins Park, Chang'an Park, Baqiao Ecological Wetland Park and Weihe Urban Green Space Sports Park have been built one after another. Looking much greener now, Xi'an, hence being honored as a "National Forest City".

古城中的绿茵——环城西苑 ◉
Green lawns in the ancient city – the
West Garden along the City Wall

自2020年以来,西安市充分利用渭河、沣河、浐河、灞河、秦岭丰富的自然山水生态和历史人文资源稳步推进"三河一山"绿道建设。

面向未来的"三河一山"绿道建设,有机串联起广域山水资源,四线围合形成超级生态廊道,标志着大西安阔步迈入"拥河发展"的新时代。一条展现西安山水资源的绿色生态廊道成为市民观光、休闲的好去处。

▽ 西安 "三河一山" 绿道
City Greenway of "Three Rivers and One Mountain" in Xi'an

Since 2020, Xi'an has made full use of the rich natural landscape ecology and historical and cultural resources of the rivers like Weihe, Fenghe and Chanhe together with the Qinling Mountains to steadily promote the construction of "Three Rivers and One Mountain" greenway.

The future-oriented greenway construction of "Three Rivers and One Mountain" organically connects broad-area landscape resources, and the four lines form a super ecological corridor, which indicates that Xi'an has entered a new era of "river-oriented development". A green ecological corridor showing the landscape resources in Xi'an became a resort for citizens' sightseeing and recreation.

"三河一山"之沣河城市绿道 ▽
City Greenway of "Three Rivers and One Mountain" on Fenghe River

● "三河一山"绿道依托渭河、沣河、浐灞河以及秦岭自然山水生态和历史人文资源，为市民呈现一条体验古都山水文化的多彩生态廊道。图为浐灞河综合改造工程

The "Three Rivers and One Mountain" greenway rely on the natural landscape ecology and historical and cultural resources of the Weihe River, Fenghe River, Chanba River and Qinling Mountains, it presents a colorful ecological corridor for citizens to experience the landscape and culture of the ancient capital. The picture shows the comprehensive reconstruction project of the Chanba River.

2020 年以来，西安开展全域治水、碧水兴城
工作，生态环境持续改善，治水成效逐步显
现。图为西安渭河城市运动公园

Since 2020, Xi'an has carried out the work of harnessing water
in the whole region and revitalizing the city with clear water.
As a result, the ecological environment has been continuously
improved, and the effect of harnessing water has gradually
appeared. The picture shows the Xi'an Weihe City Sports Park.

绿道工程西咸新区段
The Greenway Project at Xi'an-Xianyang New District

● 灞河绿道
the Bahe Greenway

2021 年以来，全域治水碧水兴城三年行动累计完成投资 306.2 亿元，260 个重点治水项目完工 160 个，渭河、灞河、沣河等实现堤防全贯通，"三河一山"环线 205 千米绿道主体已全部完工，重塑了河流生态廊道，74 千米环线绿道核心段实现了无障碍贯通；149 个绿地公园建设完成，极大改善了城市生态环境。

2021 年 7 月，目前全球最大的地下空间综合利用工程，全国最大的城市林带建设项目——幸福林带项目正式对外开放，"丝路上的城市绿洲"首次呈现在西安市民眼前。

● 西安幸福林带位于幸福路和万寿路之间，东西宽 210 米，南北长 5.85 千米，是全球最大的地下空间利用工程之一、全国最大的城市林带工程
Xi'an Happiness Forest Belt is located between Xingfu (Happiness) Road and Wanshou Road, which is 210m wide from east to west and 5.85km long from south to north. It is one of the largest underground space utilization projects in the world and the largest urban forest belt project in China.

Since 2021, the three-year operation of water control and clear water development in the whole region has completed an investment of 30.62 billion yuan, and 160 key water control projects have been completed.The enbankment of the Weihe River, the Bahe River and the Fenghe River has been fully carried out, and the main body of the 205-kilometer greenway of the "Three Rivers and One Mountain" ring line has been finished. The river ecological corridor has been reshaped, the core section of the 74-kilometer ring greenway has been barrier-free and 149 green parks have been constructed, which have greatly improved the urban ecological environment.

In July 2021, the world's largest comprehensive underground space utilization project and the country's largest urban forest belt construction project, Happiness Forest Belt Project, were officially opened to the public. As a result, "urban oasis on Silk Road" was first presented to Xi'an citizens.

西安正在大力开展城市绿化建设改造提升工作，在航天基地塬边绿带、高新区唐延路、绕城高速丈八出入口、长安区文苑路绿廊、鄠邑区体育公园、西汉高速鄠邑出入口等地进行城市绿化改造提升工作。其中，长安区文苑路绿廊改造项目形成了一条"三季有花，四季常绿"的绿色生态长廊。

Xi'an is vigorously carrying out the transformation and upgrading of urban greening construction in such areas as the tableland-side green belt at the Aerospace Base, Tangyan Road in the High-tech Zone, Zhangba Gateway of the Ring Expressway, Wenyuan Road Green Corridor in Chang'an District, Sports Park in Huyi District and Huyi Gateway of Xi'an-Hanzhong Expressway. The reconstruction project of Wenyuan Road in Chang'an District has formed a green ecological corridor with flowers in three seasons and evergreen all year round.

高新区唐延路城市绿道
City Greenway of Tangyan Road in
High-tech Zone

西安城市交通便捷，地铁纵横，目前运营线路 7 条，总通行里程位居全国第九。

西安成功创建国家公交都市示范城市。2021 年将实现西安文化中心及 17 条快速路和 10 座大型立交等立体交通建设。

西安围绕"三中心"周边交通设施和片区快速路网体系建设，陆续实施了一批放射线、三环改造、辅助环线等快速路项目。截至 2021 年 6 月，昆明路—西延路、建工路—新兴南路、体育中心外围提升改善道路一标段、二标段、会展中心外围提升改善道路、西铜高速城市段等 6 个快速路项目建成投用，其中包含 11 座立交和 7 条主要道路的快速化改造。全市新建快速路约 60 千米（含立交桥），快速路体系已初步集结成网。

2021 年 5 月 31 日，随着经九路下穿陇海铁路隧道断头路的竣工通车，标志着西安实现了全市断头路打通任务阶段性清零。

2021 年 8 月 1 日，纬零街通车。纬零街西起电子西街，东至长安南路，全长 3.2 千米，宽 50 米~60 米，双向六车道。纬零街通车有效缓解了南二环和南三环之间东西向通行压力，为一路贯通曲江、高新打下了坚实基础。

宽敞大气的地铁 2 号线钟楼站站厅
Spacious Station Hall of Zhonglou (Bell Tower) Station of Metro Line 2

Xi'an is characterized by convenient urban traffic. The total mileage of Xi'an Metro with 7 operating lines ranks ninth in China.

Xi'an has successfully established itself as a national demonstration city of public transit metropolis. In 2021, the three-dimensional transportation of Xi'an Cultural Center with17 expressways and 10 large interchanges will be completed.

Focusing on the transportation facilities around the "three centers" and the construction of expressway network system in Xi'an, a number of expressway projects such as building radiating highways, reconstructing the Third Ring Road and constructing auxiliary ring roads have been implemented one after another. By June 2021, six expressway projects, including Kunming Road-Xiyan Road, Jiangong Road-Xinxing South Road, the first and second sections of upgrading and improving the roads around the sports center, the upgrading and improvement of the roads around the convention and exhibition center and the urban section of Xitong Expressway, were completed and put into use, including the building of 11 interchanges and the rapid transformation of 7 main roads. The newly-built expressway in the whole city is about 60 kilometers (including overpass), and the expressway system has been initially assembled into a network.

On August 1, 2021, Weiling Street was opened to traffic. Weiling Street extends from Dianzi West Street in the west to Chang'an South Road in the east, with a total length of 3.2km, a width of 50m-60m and six lanes in both directions. The opening of Weiling Street has effectively eased the east-west traffic pressure between South Second Ring Road and South Third Ring Road, and laid a solid foundation for the traffic going all the way through Qujiang District and Hi-Tech Zone..

西安全力打造 10 个"15 分钟便民服务圈"，市民从居住地步行
15 分钟即可满足出行、购物、休闲等方面的基本需求。

　　Xi'an has made every effort to build 10 "15-minute convenience service
circles", and its citizens can meet their basic needs for travel, shopping and
leisure by walking for 15 minutes from their residences.

▶ 15分钟便民圈规划示意图
Schematic Diagram of 15-minute Convenience Circle Planning

▼ 会展中心旁边的口袋公园
Schematic Diagram of Convenience Circle Planning

2020 年，国家医疗中心城市，西安排名第四。西安现有三级甲等医院 27 个，在全国城市医院数量排名第 7 位、在全国城市床位数量排名第 12 位，整体名列全国前茅。空军军医大学西京医院、西安交通大学第一附属医院医疗实力居全国前列。

西安市将在三年内新增三级医院床位数 1.6 万张以上，创建 12 个国家区域医疗中心，区县级医院全部达到三级医院服务水平，建成"15 分钟医疗卫生服务圈"，让全体市民享受到更高水平、更高质量全生命周期服务，将西安打造成为西部领先、辐射周边、面向全国的高标准区域卫生健康中心。

进入新时代，西安着力深化教育综合改革。2020 年，实施基础教育提升行动，新建、改扩建学校 195 所，新增学位 19.4 万个，是西安新建学校、新增学位最多的一年。2021 年，126 所新建、改扩建学校 9 月份将全部投用，新增学位 10.8 万个。

▼ 2020 年 5 月 1 日，空军军医大学第一附属医院欢迎援鄂医疗队凯旋仪式
On May 1, 2020, the First Affiliated Hospital of Air Force Military Medical University welcomed the triumphant return of the medical aid team sent to Hubei during the Covid-19 epidemic. Photograph by Yu Juan

In 2020, Xi'an, the national medical center city, ranked fourth in China. Xi'an currently has 27 highest-level hospitals, and ranks 7th in the number of urban hospitals and 12th in the number of urban hospital beds in China, among the top on the whole. The medical strength of Xijing Hospital of Air Force Military Medical University and the First Affiliated Hospital of Xi'an Jiaotong University ranks in the forefront in China.

In three years, Xi'an will add more than 16,000 beds in tertiary hospitals, create 12 national regional medical centers, and build a "15-minute medical and health service circle", so that all citizens can enjoy higher-level and higher-quality life-cycle services, and build Xi'an into a leading regional health center in the western regions, radiating its influence into the surrounding areas and providing high-standard services to the whole country.

Entering the new era, Xi'an has made great efforts to deepen the comprehensive reform of education. In the implementation of basic education promotion plan in 2020, 195 schools were newly built, renovated and expanded, and 194,000 new seats were added. This was the year when Xi'an built the most new schools and added the largest number of new school seats.

In 2021, all 126 new, reconstructed and expanded schools will be put into use in September, with 108000 new degrees.

唐都医院 ⬤
The Hospital of Tang Du

2019 年以来，西安市全面启动"三改一通一落地"工程。目前西安老旧小区改造已完成 1861 个，惠及群众 28 万余户。电力架空线落地 72 条、235 千米，努力满足人民群众对美好生活的向往。2021 年 4 月，西安火车站北广场及周边市政配套项目全面建成交付使用。

Xi'an has vigorously carried out the project of "three renovations, one getting-through and one landing"from 2019. At present, 1861 old residential areas in Xi'an have been reconstructed, benefiting more than 280000 households.37 back streets and alleys have been upgraded and reconstructed, and 72 overhead power lines have landed for 235 kilometers, which aims to meet the people's yearning for a better life.In 2021, the north square of Xi'an railway station and its surrounding municipal supporting projects will be completed and put into use..

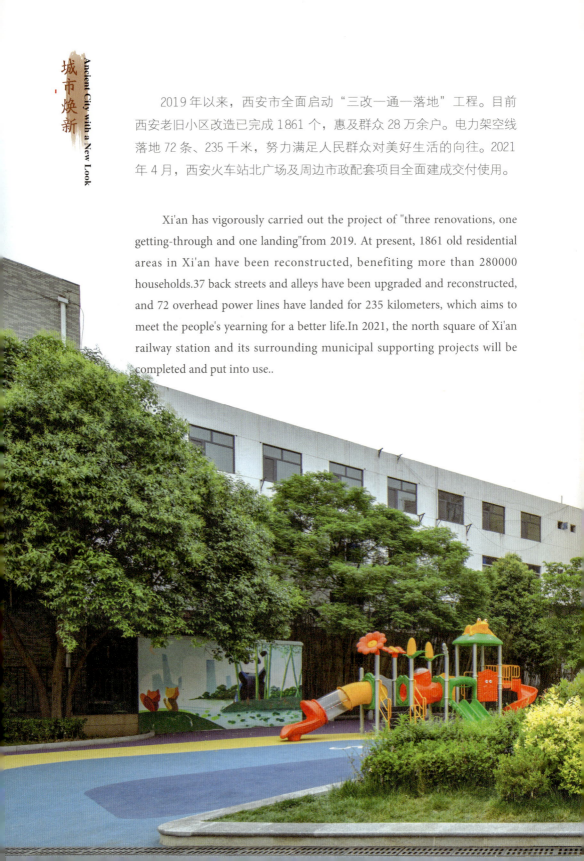

西安大力推进"书香之城"建设，目前拥有实体书店 2664 个，位居全国前四，荣获"书店之都"称号。2019 年西安成功举办第 29 届全国图书交易博览会。

Working to become a "city of books", Xi'an has 2,664 brick-and-mortar bookstores, the fourth-most in China, and it has won the title of being a "City of Bookstores". In 2019, it hosted the 29th National Book Trade Fair.

「礼赞新中国，书香新丝路」第 29 届全国图书交易博览会在西安举行

The 29th National Book Trade Fair with the theme of "Tribute to New China, Books on New Silk Road" was held in Xi'an

万邦·蓝海风漫巷书店为庆祝祖国 70 华诞举行的快闪活动

Quick Flashing held to celebrate the 70th birthday of New China at Wan Bang Bookstore

西安市民业余生活新潮时尚、丰富多彩。西安以钟楼为原点，以南北中轴线为承载，以"开元商城＋SKP购物中心＋太古里（小雁塔）片区＋小寨赛格＋曲江CCBD"为重要节点，正打造一条国际化、多业态超级商业轴线。

漫步古今交融的现代长安，传承千年历史文化，展现现代商业文明的特色美食街区、历史文化街区、时尚潮流街区，如满天繁星点缀于超级商业中轴的银河左右，缔造出西安的商业宇宙。

Xi'an residents' sparetime life is fashionable and colorful. Xi'an is building an international and multi-format super commercial axis by taking Bell Tower as the point of origin, the north-south central axis as the bearing, and "Kaiyuan Mall+SKP Shopping Center+Taikooli (Small Wild Goose Pagoda) Area+Xiaozhai SEG+Qujiang CCBD" as the important nodes.

Strolling through the modern city of Chang'an with both the ancient and the modern in perfect harmony, one can see that the city not only inherits the thousand-year history and culture, but also possessesthe quarters that present modern commercial civilization, for exmple, characteristic food blocks, history and culture blocks and fashion blocks. They are like stars dotted on both sides of the super commercial axis, creating the commercial world of Xi'an.

2019 西安城墙国际音乐节
Xi'an City Wall International Music Festival 2019

追赶超越向未来
Bright and Promising Future

　　新时代以来，党和国家进一步赋权赋能西安，高等级、全方位、多领域助推西安社会经济高质量发展。2009 年批复的《关中—天水经济区发展规划》确立了西安建设国际化大都市的总体目标，2018 年印发的《关中平原城市群发展规划》明确了西安国家中心城市的战略定位。与此同时，西安还承担着国家系统推进全面创新改革试验、中国（陕西）自贸区核心区、临空经济示范区、服务贸易、跨境贸易、电子商务、下一代互联网、国家新一代人工智能创新发展试验区等 34 项国家级试验、试点、示范任务，政策连续叠加，制度红利充沛，进一步激发出西安勇立潮头的发展活力。

In the new era, the Party and the state have entrusted Xi'an with more rights and capabilities to promote the high-quality social and economic development of Xi'an in a high-level, all-round and multi-field manner. The Guanzhong-Tianshui Economic Zone Development Plan approved in 2009 established the overall goal of building Xi'an into an international metropolis, and the Guanzhong Plain Urban Agglomeration Development Plan issued in 2018 defined the strategic orientation of Xi'an as a national central city. Meanwhile, Xi'an also undertakes 34 state-level experiment, pilot and demonstration tasks, such as the national systematic experiment to promote comprehensive innovation and reform, the core area of China (Shaanxi) Free Trade Zone, the airport economic demonstration zone, service trade, cross-border trade, e-commerce, the next generation Internet, and the national new-generation artificial intelligence innovation and development pilot zone. The policies are continuously superimposed and the institutional dividends are abundant, which can further stimulate the development vitality of Xi'an.

空中看西咸新区
Aerial view of Xi'an-Xianyang New District

2021 年 6 月 28 日，《关于印发西安市全面代管西咸新区指导意见的通知》正式印发，西咸新区直管区由西安市全面管理，加快推进西安—咸阳一体化发展进程，加快西安国家中心城市建设，优化西咸新区管理体制。

On June 28, 2021, the "Notice on Printing and Distributing the Guiding Opinions for Xi'an's Overall Escrow of Xi'an-Xianyang New District" was officially issued, and the direct administration area of Xi'an-Xianyang New District is now fully managed by Xi'an City, aiming to further accelerate the development process of Xi'an-Xianyang integration, to speed up the construction of Xi'an as a national central city and to optimize the management system of Xi'an-Xianyang New District.

西咸新区金湾俯瞰 ●
Bird's eye view of Jinwan in Xi'an-Xianyang New District

西咸新区夜景
Night view of Xi'an-Xianyang
New District

2021 年 9 月 15 日至 9 月 27 日，中华人民共和第十四届运动会将在西安隆重举行，这既是全运会首次在中国西部举行，也是西安 1949 年以来举办的规模最大的全国性赛事。适逢建党一百周年，西安紧抓国家体育赋能，充分发挥国内规格最高、规模最大、竞技水平最高、辐射带动作用最强的综合性运动会举办契机，弘扬体育文化，彰显时代精神，办好全运会，并前瞻统筹"后全运时代"城市发展，为西安注入更具活力的发展动力和价值内涵。

From September 15 to 27, 2021, the 14th National Games will be held grandly in Xi'an. It is not only the first National Games held in western China but also the largest national sports event hosted by Xi'an since 1949. Because the National Games coincides with the centenary of the founding of the Commuinist Party of China, Xi'an will take advantage of the national sports empowerment and give full play to the opportunity of holding the comprehensive sports meeting with the highest specifications, the largest scale, the highest competitive level and the strongest driving effect in China, hoping to promote sports culture, to highlight the spirit of the times and to run the National Games well. And Xi'an will also make forward-looking overall plans for urban development in the post-National Games era so as to inject more dynamic development momentum and value connotations into Xi'an.

◗ 西安奥体中心体育场内景
Interior of Xi'an Olympic Sports Center Stadium

当前，西安已确立了大西安、国家中心城市、国际化大都市"三步走"总体战略，加快推进西安—咸阳一体化进程，聚力打造"三中心两高地一枢纽"六维支撑体系，强化国家中心城市功能，辐射带动关中平原城市群，积极融入国内国际双循环新格局，为建设具有历史文化特色的国际化大都市而不断奋进。

千年古都，从长安到西安，每一帧故事都是传奇，也都将成为传奇。

At present, Xi'an has established the "three-step" overall strategy of building a larger Xi'an, a national central city and an international metropolis. It has accelerated the integration process of Xi'an and Xianyang, and made great efforts to build a six-dimensional support system of "three centers, two uplands and one hub". It has strengthened the function of the national central city, led the development of the Guanzhong Plain urban agglomeration, actively integrated into the new pattern of domestic and international double circulation, and made continuous efforts to build an international metropolis with historical and cultural characteristics.

In this ancient capital city from Chang'an to Xi'an, every single frame of its story was, is and will be a marvel.

西安奥体中心体育馆内景 ▼
Interior of Xi'an Olympic Sports Center Gymnasium

● 西安奥体中心"一场两馆"（体育场、综合体育馆、游泳跳水馆）
Xi'an Olympic Sports Center with "one stadium and two gymnasiums" (stadium, comprehensive gymnasium, swimming and diving gymnasium)

后 记

"相约西安 筑梦全运"。2021年中华人民共和国第十四届运动会在西安举办，使这里成为全国瞩目的热门城市，为城市发展带来新的契机。

西安，向下扎根是千载历史底蕴，远处扬帆是东方人文魅力。西安，背靠秦岭，生长于秦川大地，以八水为衣带，以阔步昂首之姿迈向未来，敞开粗犷厚实之胸怀迎四方来客。在西安人民不懈地努力之下，"三河一山"绿道建设焕发城市新生；大遗址公园诉说千年古都风华；文旅融合演绎时代新声；中亚班列、中欧班列沿着对外开放之路高速前行。

本书出版之年，正值中国共产党成立一百周年。百年来，党领导人民书写了中华民族几千年来的恢弘史诗，西安人民亦在党的领导下，奋发图强，锐意进取，交出一份份傲人的发展成绩单，铸就一幅幅繁荣的城市新景象。如今，西安人民永葆初心，用青山绿水绘就蓝图，用包容开放向世界展示国家中心城市风采，用坚定信念奋力谱写西安新时代追赶超越新篇章，引领城市理想生活，欢迎贵客常来长安。

本书出版过程中，受到许多单位和个人的帮助。其中，部分照片由卜杰、陈群、张颖博、刘珂、薛铂、射虎、梁冰、高江峰、李念、苟秉宸、窦翊明、王忠义、朱建强、祁海潮、谢伟、尚洪涛、王健、李伟嘉、侯新力、老猎鹰、赵晨、孙晋强、李欣、张天柱等拍摄；曲江新区管委会、高新区管委会、西咸新区管委会既各区县相关部门亦参与供图，并对本书的出版提供多种协助，在此一并感谢！

因编者能力和水平有限，本书不足之处，欢迎广大读者提出宝贵意见和建议。

Postscript

"Let's meet in Xi'an to build a dream at the National Games". The 14th Games of the People's Republic of China, which is to be held in Xi'an in 2021, will make Xi'an a popular city by attracting national attention and bringing new opportunities for its urban development.

Xi'an, deeply rooted in a thousand years of history, is sailing far and wide with its oriental humanistic charm. Xi'an, which is backed by Qinling Mountains, nurtured by the fertile land of the central Shaanxi plain and encircled by the eight beautiful rivers, is striding forward to the future with a broad and open mind to welcome visitors from all directions. With the unremitting efforts of the people of Xi'an, the construction of the "Three Rivers and One Mountain" greenway rejuvenates the city; the Great Ruins Park tells the story of the ancient capital of a millennium; the integration of culture and travel interprets the new voice of the times; the central Asia trains and China-Europe trains are advancing at a high speed along the road of opening up to the outside world.

The year when this book is published coincides with the centenary of the founding of the Communist Party of China (CPC). Over the past hundred years, the Party has led the people to write magnificent epics of the Chinese nation for thousands of years. Under the leadership of the Party, the people of Xi'an have worked hard and forged ahead, handing over impressive development transcripts and casting new scenes of a prosperous city. Nowadays, the people of Xi'an always keep their original aspirations, draw blueprints with green mountains and clean waters, show the world the brilliant style of a national central city with inclusiveness and openness, and strive to write a new chapter of Xi'an's catching up with and surpassing other cities in the new era with firm belief, thus to take a lead in creating the ideal urban life and to welcome guests to visit Chang'an frequently.

During the publication of this book, many organizations and individuals have offered us generous help. Among them, such individuals as Bu Jie, Chen Qun, Zhang Yingbo, Liu Ke, Xue Bo, She Hu, Liang Bing, Gao Jiangfeng, Li Nian, Gou Bingchen, Dou Yiming, Wang Zhongyi, Zhu Jiangqiang, Qi Haichao, Xie Wei, Shang Hongtao, Wang Jian, Li Weijia, Hou Xinli, Laolieying, Zhao chen, Sun Jinqiang, Li Xin, Zhang Tianzhu have contributed their photos, and such organizations as Qujiang New District Administrative Committee, High-tech Zone Administrative Committee, Xi'an-Xianyang New District Administrative Committee and relevant departments of all districts and counties have also participated in the contribution. Sincere thanks must be given to all of them.

Although the editors have been working very hard to make this book a success, there might still be some deficiencies. Any valuable opinions and suggestions are highly appreciated.

西安发布

西安网

悦享莲湖

长乐未央

美丽临潼

蓝田宣传

周至政务

鄠邑宣传

西安高新

曲江新区

西安航空基地

西安航天基地

西咸新区

文明西安

西安大交通发布